J.F.K.

A Hidden Life

J.F.K.

A Hidden Life

ROBIN CROSS

BLOOMSBURY

The author and publishers would like to thank the
staff of the John Fitzgerald Kennedy Library,
Columbia Point, Dorchester, Massachusetts, for
their help in selecting the illustrations for this
book. A debt of gratitude is also owed to
Charles U. Daly, of the Library, for his help and
hospitality; and also to Dave Powers for the wealth
of anecdotal information he provided about John
F. Kennedy's political career.

First published 1992
by Bloomsbury Publishing Limited
2 Soho Square, London W1V 5DE

Concept and design
© Bloomsbury Publishing Limited
Text © Robin Cross

A CIP catalogue record for this book is available
from the British Library
ISBN O 7475 1278 7

Designed and typeset by Aztec Press Limited
Printed by Butler & Tanner Limited,
Frome & London

J.F.K.

A Hidden Life

C O N T E N T S

Chapter One

Founding Fathers

*Something of Jack Kennedy's legendary
charm can be seen in this early photograph as
he poses somewhat bashfully in the guise of a
policeman.*

John Fitzgerald Kennedy came into the world on 29 May 1917 in a pleasant three-storey wood-frame house at 83 Beals Street in Brookline, Massachusetts, on the outskirts of Boston. His parents, Rose and Joseph Kennedy, already had one child, Joseph Jr, who had been born in 1915. A third child, Rosemary, was born in 1918, and she was to be followed by Kathleen (1920), Eunice (1921), Patricia (1924), Robert (1925), Jean (1928) and Edward (1932).

The Kennedy family's comfortable circumstances in the late spring of 1917, just two months after the United States had entered the First World War, were far removed from the teeming Boston stews which had sheltered John F. Kennedy's paternal great-grandfather Patrick Kennedy, who had emigrated to America from the village of Dunganstown in County Wexford in 1848.

Patrick Kennedy was the third son of a relatively prosperous farmer who grew barley and wheat on 80 acres. The tens of thousands of his fellow countrymen who in the 1840s took the same hazardous passage across the Atlantic were for the most part less fortunate peasants, oppressed by absentee landlords and uprooted by the potato blight. In the four years from 1845 which saw the Great Hunger, a million Irish died and a million more left their homeland. Those who headed West could sail to New York or Boston for as little as $12.

Conditions on the "coffin ships" which carried them came close to rivaling the horrors of the slavers of the eighteenth century. In 1847 disease claimed 20 per cent of those who set out. Boston's harbor master claimed that he could detect the approach of the immigrant ships, when they were still miles out to sea, by the pestilential stench which the winds bore before them.

WANTED—A good, reliable woman to take the care of a boy two years old, in a small family in Brookline. Good wages and a permanent situation given. No washing or ironing will be required, but good recommendations as to character and capacity demanded. Positively no Irish need apply. Call at 224 Washington street, corner of Summer street. jy 28 6t

Above: An example of the discrimination against the Irish in Boston, which continued well into the twentieth century. Right: Conditions on the ships which brought the "famine Irish" to America bred disease and killed thousands of emigrants before they reached the promised land.
Opposite: "P. J." Kennedy in 1887, his confident gaze and bristling moustache recalling Theodore Roosevelt. In the previous year, at the age of twenty-eight, he had begun the first of five consecutive terms in the Massachusetts House of Representatives.

The great wave of human flotsam which washed into Boston increased the city's population by nearly 50 per cent in the 1840s. Many of the so-called "famine Irish" stayed in the waterlocked city, too poor to travel any further. Confined to thousands of typhus-ridden tenements in a hundred Mick Alleys and Paddyvilles, they were condemned to a life as nasty, brutish and short as the one they had left behind in Ireland. The Boston Brahmins, the native-born Anglo-Saxon *haute bourgeoisie* who were the arbiters of the city's cultural life and the controllers of its financial and mercantile activity, recoiled in horror from the immigrant invasion. They initiated a form of apartheid which, at its most basic level, found expression in the notorious signs which read NINA – "No Irish Need Apply". Mayor Theodore Lyman declared that the Irish were "a race that will never be infused with our own, but on the contrary will always remain distant and hostile". For their own part the Irish avoided assimilation, not least because of the Protestant bias of the city's public schools.

Patrick Kennedy was one of those who stayed in Boston, finding employment as a cooper. He made yokes and staves for the broad-wheeled covered wagons which rumbled off to join the California Gold Rush, and whiskey barrels for the waterfront saloons which provided the Irish with some distraction from their harsh lot.

Even more important for the tightly knit and inward-looking Irish community was the

family. Transplanted from rural to urban poverty, the Irish maintained the tradition of the extended family as a deep emotional support and means of economic survival.

In 1849 Patrick Kennedy married twenty-eight-year-old Bridget Murphy, a fellow steerage passenger on the voyage to America. By 1858 there were four children, three girls and a son; the youngest, Patrick Joseph, was born on 14 January of that year. Ten months later his father died of cholera, leaving Bridget to raise her children on the money she earned as a hairdresser and the income from a small store she owned.

Patrick Joseph, or "PJ" as he became known as he grew up, spent his teenage years working on the Boston wharves as a stevedore. At the age of twenty-two he bought a small, run-down saloon in Haymarket Street. Industrious, ambitious and teetotal, he prospered, acquired other saloons, moved into retail and wholesale whiskey distribution and then into politics. Politics was the great Irish success story in Boston. Quarantined in their shanty towns, excluded from the professions and polite society and ignored by the existing civic institutions, which were indifferent to their grievances against predatory employers and rapacious landlords, the Irish created their own parallel political "machine". What began as a strategy of necessity provided a route to power and prestige which even the old Boston elite could not deny the unwanted newcomers.

"PJ's" position as a saloonkeeper, the

Opposite: John F. Fitzgerald, known to everyone in Boston as "Honey Fitz", and "P.J." Kennedy (right), powerful allies in the jungle of Boston politics and founders of a dynasty whose influence is still felt today. Below: A family gathering on Orchard Beach, Maine, in 1908. "P.J.", second on the left, relaxes next to the young Rose Fitzgerald. "Honey Fitz" is on her left while the handsome young Joe Kennedy is last but one on the right.

shrewd and sympathetic listener on the other side of the bar, eased him into an influential position in the world of political clubs which were the basis of Irish politics in Boston's wards, each of which was controlled by a "boss" whose powers of patronage secured the loyalty of his supporters.

By the mid-1880s the Irish controlled Boston politics. In 1886 "PJ" and his allies took over the Democratic Committee of Ward Two in East Boston. That year "PJ" began the first of five consecutive terms in the Massachusetts House of Representatives. In 1892 he ran successfully for the State Senate and was re-elected twice. However, "PJ's" natural habitat was his ward in East Boston, where from the back room of his saloon he dispensed liquor and favors in the classic style

of such legendary "bosses" as Martin Lomasney, with whom "PJ" sat on the unofficial "Board of Strategy", based in the old Quincy House on Brattle Street.

Pulling the levers of power and patronage alongside Lomasney and "PJ" on the Board of Strategy was the North End's John F. Fitzgerald, whose charm and loquacity were to earn him the nickname of "Honey Fitz". The third son of an upwardly mobile North End shopkeeper, "Honey Fitz" graduated from the Boston Latin School and attended Harvard Medical School for a year before his father's death forced him to become the family's breadwinner. His extravagant nature, warm tongue and glad hand soon launched him on a political career as a US congressman and, in 1905, he became the first Irish Mayor of

Boston. His sheer *joie de vivre* was infectious. He celebrated his fiftieth birthday by sprinting a hundred yards at seven in the morning, running a quarter of a mile at nine, wrestling at noon and boxing at one.

"Honey Fitz" had come a long way from the tenement apartment on Ferry Street where he had begun life, but he remained only semi-detached from his "shanty" origins. The city's bluebloods admired his tireless boosting of a "Bigger, Better, Busier Boston", and joined in the general public merriment at his longstanding affair with a blonde cigarette girl, "Toodles" Ryan. Some of them might even have voted for him. None of them forgot he was Irish. "Honey Fitz" might attempt to assimilate on horseback, playing polo and riding to hounds, but this only earned him the derisive tag of "greenblood". When in 1916 the irrepressible "Honey Fitz" challenged Henry Cabot Lodge for a Senate seat, the political establishment heaved a collective sigh of relief at his defeat.

The light of "Honey Fitz's" life was the first of his six children, Rose Elizabeth, who had been educated in Europe and was the belle of Irish Boston. On holiday in Maine as a youngster, she met for the first time Joseph Patrick Kennedy, "PJ's" firstborn. In their late teens they were to meet again and fall in love. On 7 October 1914 the Kennedys and the Fitzgeralds were united when Joseph Patrick Kennedy married "Honey Fitz's" beautiful daughter.

Red-haired and supremely confident, with

Left: Joseph P. Kennedy and Rose Fitzgerald on their wedding day, 7 October 1914. They were married by Cardinal O'Connell in his private chapel. After a two-week honeymoon in White Sulphur Springs, West Virginia, the young couple moved into a frame house on Beals Street in the comfortable, middle-class, and Protestant, Boston suburb of Brookline. Within five years the first four of their children were born there.

Right: Joe Kennedy, well on the way to fulfilling his ambition to become a "millionaire by the time I'm thirty-five", a task accomplished with time to spare.

piercing blue eyes and a flashing smile, young Joe Kennedy was already shaking the Irish dust off his trouser cuffs. Educated at the Boston Latin School and Harvard, he acquired the language and ways of the Brahmins but not their wholehearted acceptance,

Joe Kennedy had displayed an early entrepreneurial flair as an undergraduate, making $5,000 out of a sightseeing bus he ran to Lexington and Concord. After graduating from Harvard he went into banking as a state examiner, a job which gave him an insight into money-making and the web of connections which underlie the surface of the business world. Initially, "Honey Fitz" had been opposed to Rose marrying Joe, convinced that there was a more advantageous match to be made. But in 1913 Joe Kennedy exploited a takeover battle between a small "Irish" bank in Boston, the Columbia Trust, and a "downtown" bank, First National, to ease himself into the presidency of the Columbia Trust. At the age of twenty-five, he had become the youngest bank president in the country, an early example of Joe's genius for hype which left many in awe of the precocious financial genius and broke down "Honey Fitz's" resistance to the marriage.

Joe's delared intention was to be a millionaire by the time he was thirty-five. In later years his baseball captain at Harvard, Charles "Chuck" McLaughlin, recalled the essential Joe Kennedy: "Joe was the kind of guy who, if he wanted something bad enough, would get it, and he didn't much mind how he got it. He'd run right over anybody!" Joe very badly wanted to be rich.

At the twentieth reunion of his Harvard class, Joe listed his profession as "capitalist". But he had little respect for fellow-capitalists. He once told Joe Jr and Jack, "Big businessmen are the most overrated men in the country. Here I am, a boy from East Boston, and I took 'em. So don't be impressed."

But it was hard not to be impressed by the rise of Joe Kennedy. When the United States entered the First World War he did not volunteer for military service but took on the management of the huge Fore River shipyard in Quincy, making a tidy sum on the side by running his own canteen for the 22,000 workforce. In 1922, after a short stint in the stock department of the Boston investment banker Hayden Stone and Company, he set up on his own as "Joseph P. Kennedy, Banker".

In business Joe Kennedy remained a loner. Essentially a predator, screened by a small staff of loyal Boston-Irish utility men, he spotted opportunities, moved in, made a killing and then moved on. He was one of the most ruthless operators of "stock pools" in the 1920s, driving up the price of idle stock and then selling at the top of the market and leaving the suckers to take the losses. By Joe Kennedy's thirty-fifth birthday, the stock market and a string of lucrative real estate deals had made him not just a millionaire but a multimillionaire. Prohibition provided him with another opportunity as a bootlegger, closely linked with mobster Frank Costello.

Wealth did not buy Joe social acceptance by the Brahmins; he was blackballed when he applied for membership of the Cohasset Country Club, the summer watering hole of many old Boston families. He never forgot or forgave these slights, stranded as he was in the emotional limbo between the desire to shrug off his origins and the contempt he felt for the patricians who barred his way because, " I was an Irish Catholic and son of a barkeep. You can go to Harvard and it doesn't mean a damn thing. The only thing these people understand is money."

In 1926 Joe Kennedy moved to New York, where the real money was. The family was installed in a large house in Riverdale-on-Hudson while Joe set out to conquer a new world – Hollywood. That year he used the banking house of Hayden Stone and Company to acquire the FBO (Film Booking Offices of America) studio, a modest movie outfit whose principal products were low-budget program fillers.

Opposite: A hint of the sibling rivalry between Joe Jr (left) and Jack hangs over this holiday photograph. Rose later recalled, "Joe was much stronger than Jack, and if there was a physical encounter, Joe really whacked him, so when they were young everybody was trying to protect Jack ... Jack was a little different from Joe in that Jack always had a pal with him. I think Joe was more like me – he'd just as soon travel alone."

The movie business fascinated Joe Kennedy. He had a natural flair for public relations and admired the Hollywood moguls, for the most part bigoted vulgarians with no pretensions to culture, but, nevertheless, the masters of the mysterious alchemy which fed the American public's insatiable appetite for "stars". The mediocre FBO product interested Joe less than the process of image-making and the creation of a world of impossible glamor in which a shop-girl could be transformed into a love goddess or a factory hand turned into the fantasy lover for millions of women. It was the looming image on the screen and in the fan magazines which attracted him, not the banal reality which lay behind it. As he later told Jack, "It's not what you are that counts, but what people think you are." Jack, too, was to share his father's preoccupation with the pleasures and potential uses of Hollywood glamor.

For Joe Kennedy the pursuit of pleasure led to a long affair with Gloria Swanson, then the most successful and highly paid actress of the silent screen. In 1928 they embarked on an independent production, Queen Kelly, which foundered on the extravagance of its director Erich von Stroheim. A million-dollar paean to sado-masochism, Queen Kelly could not be released in the United States. It was Joe Kennedy's first failure. According to Swanson he reacted "like a wounded animal whimpering in a trap".

To a man possessed by such a success drive, failure could not be contemplated. Joe once told journalist Arthur Krock, "For the Kennedys it is the shit house or castle — nothing in between". Failure on the scale of Queen Kelly could plunge Kennedy and his family back into the shit house from which his ancestors came, his ears ringing with the mocking laughter of the Brahmins. Each new financial coup was another step toward the castle to which he aspired. It was typical of Kennedy, however, that the costs of von Stroheim's folly were finally borne almost in their entirety by Gloria Swanson. Their affair ended when she discovered that the gifts of furs and jewelry he had given her had been charged to her account.

Joe Kennedy made a profitable withdrawal from the movie business when he masterminded a merger of RCA's interest in the studio with the Keith-Albee-Orpheum circuit of vaudeville houses. The result was a giant $300 million corporation from which sprang the RKO studio. He returned to the stock market, making a new fortune from the frenzied trading which preceded the Wall Street Crash of October 1929 and then short-selling as the market fell apart. It was estimated that he was now worth at least $100 million, and it was in 1929 that he established trust funds which were eventually to provide each of his children with $10 million. If money had been his overriding passion, it would not be theirs. He had extracted sufficient from his fellow-capitalists to ensure that his family was kept from any further contact with them.

In this busy year Joe Kennedy acquired two new homes: a Georgian mansion set in six acres in the staunchly Republican district of Bronxville, and a rambling, green-shuttered house at Hyannis Port, Massachusetts, on Nantucket Sound, which became the Kennedys' summer home. (In 1933 he bought a winter retreat in Florida, a Spanish-style mansion on fashionable North Ocean Boulevard in Palm Beach.)

The Kennedys needed the space. There were now eight children and the last, Edward, arrived three years later. The children were raised in an atmosphere of intense competition and ceaseless activity. Eunice later remembered her father's approach to the non-stop summer routine of tennis, soft-ball, swimming and sailing which filled the days at Hyannis Port: "... if we won he got terribly enthusiastic. Daddy was always very competitive. The thing he kept telling us was that coming second was just no good."

The pattern never changed. Many years later Dave Hackett, a Kennedy family friend and Director of the President's Committee on Juvenile Delinquency and Youth Crime during Jack's presidency, described the Kennedy approach to touch football on the Hyannis lawn: "Its 'touch' but it's murder. If you don't want to play, don't come. If you do come, play, or you'll be fed in the kitchen and no one will speak to you. Don't let the girls fool you. Even pregnant they can make you look silly. If Harvard played touch, they'd be on the varsity ... Run madly on every play and make a lot of noise. Don't appear to be having too

Jack, Rosemary, Kathleen and Eunice.

much fun, though. They'll accuse you of not taking the game seriously enough ... Don't criticize the other team either. It's bound to be full of other Kennedys too, and the Kennedys don't like that sort of thing ... To be really popular you must show raw guts."

Joe's strictures bore down most heavily on Jack and his older brother Joe Jr. The two boys presented a sharp contrast. Joe Jr took after his father, athletic, daring, short-tempered, but with bags of ready charm radiating from his square, open face. His dazzling smile could change instantly to a steely glare in imitation of the baleful, crushing look with which his father maintained discipline. Joe Jr was the star of the family, in

whom reposed hopes of a great future. Even in his teenage years he was talked of as the first Irish president of the United States. He breezily told the socialist academic Harold Laski as much, when studying under him at the London School of Economics in 1933. During Joe Kennedy's frequent, lengthy absences Joe Jr acted as the little ones' surrogate father.

Between Joe Jr and Jack there was a fierce rivalry in which the latter could rarely prevail. Jack was a sickly child, tormented by allergies, often ill and in hospital, and suffering pain from what a doctor was to call "an unstable back". Like a true Kennedy he never complained. Bobby once joked,

"...When we were growing up together we used to laugh about the great risk a mosquito took in biting Jack Kennedy – with some of his blood the mosquito was almost sure to die."

Tussles between Jack and Joe Jr frequently ended in blows. Although Jack fought tigerishly, he nearly always came off second best. When the two boys raced each other round the block on their bicycles in opposite directions, neither gave way and they collided head-on. Jack needed twenty-eight stitches; Joe strolled away without a scratch. During fiercely contested sailing races at Hyannis Port, Joe Jr frequently threw Jack overboard for sloppy sailing.

Confined to bed for long spells, Jack turned his naturally quick and curious mind to voracious reading. The socialite and author Kay Halle, an old friend of the Kennedy family, caught a revealing glimpse of Jack Kennedy at the age of fifteen: "Joseph Kennedy Sr asked me if I would stop with him while we were in the hospital to see his young son who was in there quite ill. I think he had a football injury, and that was the first time I saw Jack Kennedy. We went into his bedroom, his room at the hospital, and you could hardly see him, he was so buried in the bed under masses of books. All I could see was this peaked little face with freckles standing out on the bridge of his nose – his pale little face – and I was awfully interested because the book he was reading was *World Crisis* by Winston Churchill."

The Kennedy family was a society in miniature, created in Joe's image and sustained by his willpower, even if it was often exercised at long distance. A Bronxville neighbor remembered: "Pat and Eunice were always saying 'Dad says this' and 'Dad says that'. But if I hadn't finally met him I never would have known he existed." Even when he was away they conformed to the pattern he had drilled into them, working and playing together as a team.

Sadly, there was one member of the family who could not keep up. Long before she reached adolescence it was clear that Rosemary was retarded. Rose tried to cushion her with a routine of normality, but Rosemary could only sit on the sidelines as her siblings hurtled around Hyannis Port or sailed off into the bay. As she grew older Rosemary became thick-set and prone to violent tantrums; on one terrible occasion flying at the elderly "Honey Fitz". She was sent away to special schools, from where her letters to her father, full of fractured spelling, eerie ellipses and childish endearments, strike a note of great sadness. In 1941, without consulting Rose or any of the family, Joe authorized a pre-frontal lobotomy for Rosemary which reduced the poor young woman to a shell.

The family refused publicly to admit Rosemary's handicap. After the lobotomy she was sent to a nursing convent in Wisconsin, and until the 1960s the Kennedys maintained the fiction that she was a shy woman whose vocation was nursing mentally retarded children. Rose and Eunice visited her regularly, but for Joe dropping out of the charmed family circle was akin to death. In later years he could barely bring himself to talk of Rosemary. His daughter was a "loser", and losing could not be forgiven.

Rosemary exposed the fault lines in the Kennedy family. Beneath the frantic activity, and Joe's relentless character-building regime at Hyannis Port, there was a perceptible air of rootlessness and emotional dislocation. A guest visiting Hyannis Port was surprised to discover that the children did not have rooms of their own but, when visiting, were billeted in whichever bedrooms were available. Nor was their parents' marriage an entirely happy one. Joe's sexual behavior was as predatory as his business methods; when Joe Jr and Jack were a little older none of their dates was safe from his nocturnal molestations. He had humiliated Rose by insisting that Gloria Swanson accompany them on a return sea voyage from Europe. Rose submitted with a kind of weird calm, prompting Gloria to reflect, "Was she a fool ... or a saint? Or just a better actress than I was?"

Rose reconciled herself to Joe's mistresses, consoling herself with regular trips to the Paris fashion houses and a domestic regime which mixed extreme religiosity with distracted eccentricity as she stalked through the Kennedy homes in a housecoat on which were pinned scrawled notes reminding her of the day's duties. Rose was far from the benign organizing figure of legend, famous for the card index she kept on her children's health

Joe Jr, second from left in the front row, and Jack, far right front row, both played for the football team at the Dexter School in Brookline. Jack's youthful enthusiasm for sports, the sine qua non of the Kennedy ethic, was characterized more by determination and sheer courage than skill.

problems. She left a kind of emptiness where she passed. Later, in an unguarded moment, Jack bitterly confided that when he needed her his mother was "on her knees praying all over Europe".

Joe was the psychic architect of the boys' lives, encouraging them to be privately cynical about their Catholic faith, to acknowledge their "Irishness" only when it was of practical advantage, to adopt a candidly rapacious attitude toward women, and to win at all costs. While the boys were deliberately not sent to Catholic schools (to help them learn early on how to mix in a wider world), the girls underwent an ultra-orthodox Catholic education. The boys were to fulfil their destiny by bearing the Kennedy standard into public affairs. The girls' role was to attract capable husbands whom marriage would transmogrify into "honorary Kennedys" whose task it would be to serve as loyal staffers for the Kennedy sons' careers. And of course they would all produce lots more Kennedys. Joe had it all worked out.

He was also working on his own political career. After the Wall Street Crash Joe Kennedy had gauged the seismic shift it produced in American society and become an important supporter of Franklin Delano Roosevelt in his campaign for the presidency. There was little or no ideological basis to Joe's commitment to Roosevelt – he was a Democrat by Boston-Irish tradition rather than conviction – merely the drive for achievement in a new field, the expectation that his loyalty

would be rewarded and the underlying belief that Roosevelt's policies stood the best chance of preventing the social upheavals which might threaten the Kennedy fortune.

Joe Kennedy was a key fixer in FDR's successful bid for the Democratic nomination in 1932 and in the campaign which followed. But when Roosevelt entered the White House, Kennedy was passed over for high office. Disgruntled, he returned to money-making. Taking advantage of the imminent repeal of Prohibition, he became the exclusive American agent for Haig and Haig and Dewar's whiskey and Gordon's gin. However, he was too large and too loose a cannon to be left slithering around the Democratic deck indefinitely. Having refused the ambassadorship to Ireland, which he clearly saw as an unwelcome form of political typecasting, Joe Kennedy accepted the chairmanship of the Securities and Exchange Commission, a central New Deal agency which had been established to clean up and supervise the stock market. Roosevelt had "set a thief to catch a thief".

Kennedy served on the SEC from July 1934 to the summer of 1935, renting a big Maryland estate overlooking the Potomac, reveling in his closeness to the center of power and the Washington social whirl. Roosevelt was a frequent guest, sipping Joe's Haig and Haig and watching unreleased movies flown in specially from Hollywood.

During this period Kennedy made maximum use of his position to woo influential press barons, perhaps the most important of

whom was the staunchly Republican Henry Luce, owner of an empire which included, Time, Life and Fortune magazines. In 1937 he had sufficient influence with Luce to secure the scrapping of a highly critical Fortune cover story and its replacement with a flattering one. It was one of many favors Luce was to pay him. In turn, Joe Kennedy took on Luce's son Hank, fresh out of college, as his special assistant on the SEC.

After resigning the chairmanship of the SEC, Joe Kennedy embarked on a fact-finding tour of Europe accompanied by Rose, Kathleen (nicknamed "Kick") and Jack. That summer the eighteen-year-old Jack had graduated from the Choate School at Wallingford, Connecticut. At Choate Jack was still living in the shadow cast by Joe Jr, who had been campus leader at Choate and a football star with a reputation as a solid student. Jack had not distinguished himself academically and had an erratic disciplinary record which he mitigated with an abundance of charm. His headmaster, George St John, reflected, "Psychologically I was enormously interested. I couldn't see how two boys from the same family could be so different ... You know in dealing with Jack, you needed a little wit as well as a little seriousness. Jack didn't like to be too serious; he had a delightful sense of humor, always... in any school he would have got away with some things, just on his smile. He was a very likeable person, very lovable."

Joe Jr had gone on to Harvard after

Above: Jack, on the right, cuts a dash at Choate. Right: Jack graduates from Choate in 1935. He went to England that summer to study at the London School of Economics, but an attack of jaundice cut short his stay and he returned to the United States.

Above: Juggling Jack, a moment of fun during JFK's trip to Europe in 1937, on which he was accompanied by Lem Billings. Opposite: Jack's frail good looks are caught by the camera on the same trip. During his time in Europe Jack arrived at the conclusion that "Fascism is the thing for Germany and Italy. Communism for Russia and England".

Choate; asserting his independence, Jack chose Princeton. His father, determined that Jack should make good use of the summer before college, sent him to London to study under Harold Laski, as Joe Jr had done. Joe had no time for Laski's socialism, but the political scientist had an international reputation and a spell sitting at his feet would look good on Jack's curriculum vitae. But almost immediately after his arrival in London Jack fell ill with jaundice and had to return home. A recurrence of the illness in the winter of 1935 cut short his time at Princeton. When he recovered he went to Harvard.

Jack's first two years at Harvard mirrored his days at Choate. Sports, in which his drive was greater than his skill, took up much of his time. His lifelong friend Torbert Macdonald recalled: "Jack and I were never too far apart. I weighed maybe 175 when I was a Freshman, and Jack couldn't have weighed more than 150 or 160. In those days you had to play [football] both ways, and he was great on offense and could tackle very well on defense, but as far as blocking and that sort of thing, where size mattered, he was under quite a handicap. Guts is the word. He had plenty of guts."

Jack seemed more interested in chasing girls – gaining an early reputation as a ladykiller – than in the events unfolding in Europe and the problems into which the New Deal was running at home. However, about halfway through his time at Harvard he became more intellectually engaged, partly because of a trip he made to Europe in the

summer of 1937 accompanied by his old schoolfriend K. LeMoyne ("Lem") Billings. They roughed it, as Lem's family was not wealthy, and Jack busied himself with sending reports to his father on what they had seen and what people had told them about the growing threat posed by Nazi Germany. In Munich the two young men devised their own uniquely American riposte to Sieg-heiling stormtroopers, raising their hands and laconically drawling "Hi ya, Hitler". From the Spanish border, where Jack interviewed Loyalist refugees, he wrote to his father of "the almost complete ignorance 95 per cent of the people in the US have about the situation as a whole here".

Jack's new interest in foreign affairs coincided with his father's appointment as US ambassador to the Court of St James, the most prestigious post in the diplomatic service. Joe had worked tirelessly for FDR's re-election in 1936, even publishing a book, *Why I'm for Roosevelt*, ghosted by Arthur Krock. But high office again eluded him and he was forced to accept the chairmanship of the Maritime Commission, from which he resigned after only a few months.

Joe had lobbied hard for the ambassadorship, eager to be at the center of things in Europe. He had confessed that he was "intrigued by the thought of being the first Irishman to be Ambassador for the United States to the Court of St James".

Roosevelt's initial reaction was one of amusement, principally at the thought of the

bandy-legged Kennedy presenting his credentials at Buckingham Palace dressed in the traditional knee breeches and stockings. But then he, too, became intrigued by the idea and, perhaps stimulated by its unorthodoxy, confirmed Joe Kennedy as the new ambassador on 9 December 1937.

In April 1938, less than a month after presenting his credentials – he had been excused the knee breeches for the ceremony – Joe and Rose were guests of the King and Queen at Windsor Castle. "Shit house or castle" had been his watchwords, and now they were savoring the splendors of one of the most famous castles in the world. Rose wrote, somewhat disingenuously: "I thought I must be dreaming that I, Rose Kennedy, a simple young matron, am really here at Windsor Castle, guest of the Queen and the little Princesses." Joe put it more pithily: "Well, Rose, this is a hell of a long way from East Boston."

The Making of a Hero

*Striding out in London in 1938, the new US
ambassador and five of his children. From
left to right, Kathleen, Joe Kennedy, Edward,
Rose, Patricia, Jean and Robert.*

Joe Kennedy created a mild sensation when he arrived in London to take up his appointment as ambassador to the Court of St James. For the British press, which he immediately began to cultivate as assiduously as he had the publishing empires at home, the new ambassador was a godsend. Dubbed "the USA's nine-child envoy", he seemed to embody every English notion of rugged American individualism, receiving reporters at the palatial embassy at 9 Queen's Gate with his feet on the desk, shooting a hole-in-one on his first day on the golf course and calling the Queen "a cute trick".

The Kennedy family provided equally good copy, and the newspapers were filled with accounts of their sorties into British society. The seventeen-year-old "Kick", in particular, was soon at home in a circle of aristocratic friends. Fears that the new ambassador might prove an Anglophobe were unfounded. Indeed, it soon became apparent that Joe Kennedy enjoyed mixing with British high society. He became a regular visitor at Cliveden, the country house presided over with erratic brilliance by his fellow-American Nancy Astor. Roosevelt mused, "Who would have thought that the English would take into camp a red-headed Irishman?" For the rest of his life Joe Kennedy liked to be referred to as "the ambassador".

He quickly established a close working relationship with the British Prime Minister Neville Chamberlain. Kennedy shared Chamberlain's belief that despite the grimmer aspects of Nazi Germany, its leader was a man with whom the democracies could reach an accommodation. In the autumn of 1938 the ambassador came out as a strong defender of the Munich agreement, having already opened up secret talks with the German envoy in Britain, Herbert von Dirksen, who cabled to Berlin that Kennedy "understood our Jewish policy completely". (In 1949 the State Department released a large number of German diplomatic messages which had been previously classified, among them von Dirksen's cables about his meetings with Joe Kennedy. The ambassador dismissed the subsequent accusations of anti-Semitism as "complete poppycock".)

Back at home Roosevelt was pursuing a policy of studied ambivalence, his room for maneuver limited by the Neutrality Acts and strong isolationist opinion. Determined to play what amounted to a policy-making role in the European crisis, Kennedy decided to thrust himself into the interstices opened up by FDR's caution. He saw himself as a kind of super-ambassador who would prevent war with initiatives of his own. At the same time Kennedy had his eye cocked on the Democratic nomination in 1940. The two-term-tradition appeared to bar Roosevelt's re-election for a third term and offered Kennedy a chance to tilt at the highest office. In the summer of 1938 *Liberty* magazine ran an article which asked, "Will Joe Kennedy Run for President?"

Like Chamberlain, the ambassador had a deep fear of war. It owed little to the collective

Joe Jr, the ambassador and Jack. Although Joe Jr was still the dominant figure among the Kennedy children, Jack was fast catching up. Jack's lifelong friend Torbert Macdonald recalled, "Joe had a sort of protective feeling towards Jack ... But Jack was very stubborn in a quiet way: the more someone would tell him he shouldn't do something, the less likely he would be to give it up."

shudder which shook the spines of Europeans when they contemplated the horrors of the Western Front. Rather, it flowed from his apprehension that a similar cataclysm would destroy the peaceful pursuit of profit. In large measure the ambassador saw the possibility of war as a personal threat to himself, his family and his fortune. These instinctive reactions strengthened his own isolationism and determination to keep America out of any European war. He was no pacifist, indeed he believed that America should be armed to the teeth to meet any threat. By the same token he was convinced that the failure of the British and the French to re-arm against the dictators with sufficient speed and in sufficient measure meant that any rapid mobilization would force them to abandon democracy and adopt totalitarian disciplines themselves, perhaps opening the door to Communism.

In 1939 Jack Kennedy took six months off from his studies at Harvard to travel in Europe and the Middle East and to act as his father's courier in Britain. Just as his father had been, the shy and immature young man was captivated by the casual elegance and detachment of members of the British upper class, like the Ormsby-Gores, with whom he became friendly, and William Cavendish, Marquess of Hartington, whose father was the tenth Duke of Devonshire. "Billy" Hartington would marry Kathleen Kennedy in 1944. These aristocrats seemed altogether more sophisticated and confident than Jack's American contemporaries. Their approach to

politics was lighthearted but, as David Nunnerly observed in his book President Kennedy and Britain, "this very idea of politics invigorating rather than dominating society much appealed to Kennedy". As President, Jack's Anglophilia was expressed in the particularly close relationship he enjoyed with the British Prime Minister Harold Macmillan. On the surface, the two men were a picture in opposites – the handsome young American and the elderly English gentleman trailing Edwardian raffishness. However, for Jack, Macmillan was to become something of a father figure – an ironic, kindly substitute for the harsh Joe Kennedy.

Twenty years earlier, Jack Kennedy came under the influence of two books: *The Young Melbourne*, David Cecil's biography of Lord Melbourne, Queen Victoria's worldy, witty and adored Prime Minister; and John Buchan's autobiography, *Pilgrim's Way*. Cecil's limpid description of Melbourne's life and political career seems, in retrospect, like a fantasy projection of Jack's own trajectory – blending bookishness with affairs of state and supported by a family "raised in gay and patrician surroundings" who would always unite against outsiders. The Kennedys were not patrician in the true sense of the word, but Joe's remarkable rise and driving regime had made the family an aristocracy unto themselves.

Cecil characterized Melbourne as a late developer, "the sort of character that in any circumstances does not come of age until

Joe Jr, Kathleen and Jack in London. The vibrant Kathleen quickly found herself at the centre of a circle of beguiling British aristocrats whose charm exercised an important influence over JFK's later style as a politician.

middle life. His nature was composed of such diverse elements that it took a long time to fuse them into a stable whole". In Jack's case the way to maturity was for many years blocked by the dominating figure of his father. A small incident in the postwar years reveals the thrall in which Jack was held. In his days as a Congressman Jack took a girlfriend to Hyannis Port while his father was away. As she watched him sitting behind the wheel of Joe's Cadillac convertible, putting the top up and down, she felt he looked "like a kid without a license, not daring to drive it on the highway".

If Cecil's book was an eerie prophesy of the Anglophile image Jack Kennedy would later fashion for himself, Buchan's book stimulated Jack's fascination with the British upper class, which he was encountering for the first time. *Pilgrim's Way* is largely a celebration of the outriders of Empire, classically educated, laconic and tough, of whom one of the great exemplars was T.E. Lawrence, not then the complicated, compromised figure he cuts today. In *The Kennedy Imprisonment*, Garry Wills highlights a passage in *Pilgrim's Way* which describes Lawrence in terms with which the young Jack Kennedy could easily identify: "Physically he looked slight, but, as boxers say, he stripped well, and he was as strong as many people twice his size, while he had a bodily toughness and endurance far beyond anything I have ever met. In 1920 his whole being was in grave disequilibrium. You

cannot in any case be nine times wounded, four times in an air crash, have many bouts of fever and dysentery, and finally at the age of twenty-nine take Damascus at the head of an Arab army, without living pretty near the edge of your strength." To a young man whose own body was in constant disequilibrium, and whose upbringing had encouraged him to live at the edge of his slight strength, T.E. Lawrence must have seemed the perfect role model. When Jack Kennedy was courting Jacqueline Bouvier he presented her with a copy of *Pilgrim's Way*.

As war approached in Europe, Joe Kennedy's honeymoon period with the British press and public, and with his own president, was running out. The rough and ready ways which had at first charmed his hosts now attracted increasing criticism. It was rumored that he had used inside information to make a share killing during the Munich crisis; his womanizing attracted unfavorable comment. The ambassador's isolationism was becoming more dogmatic at precisely the moment that Roosevelt was readying himself to cast his lot with the democracies. And his position was further undermined by his evident political ambitions and casual anti-Semitism. When war came in September 1939, he found himself on the sidelines as Roosevelt opened close personal communications with Winston Churchill, the First Lord of the Admiralty. When on 10 May 1940 Churchill became Prime Minister, Joe Kennedy's personal

Jack shared the ambassador's fascination with Hollywood and the art of image-making. Here he meets Margaret Sullavan, squired by a youthful Robert Stack, at Universal Studios in 1940.

isolation was complete. Bitterness became sour defeatism after the fall of France, and during the first month of the Blitz the ambassador spent much of his time at his home near Windsor, safe from the Luftwaffe's bombs.

Roosevelt was elected for an unprecedented third term in November 1940, a month after Joe Kennedy had returned to America rather than face the inevitability of recall. His departure was not mourned by the British establishment that he had once so ardently courted. Lord Halifax, then Foreign Secretary and ironically a "Man of Munich", circulated a Foreign Office

memorandum which dismissed Kennedy as "a very foul specimen of a double-crosser and defeatist". He remained unrepentant in his isolationism and dissipated much of his dwindling political capital when, in an interview he gave the Boston Globe, he claimed that "democracy in England is finished". The ensuing uproar put an end to his own political ambitions.

The fourteen months since the outbreak of war had proved an unmitigated disaster for the ambassador. But he had ensured that they were an unqualified triumph for his son Jack. Jack had graduated from Harvard *cum laude* in political science in June 1940. He had drawn on his experiences in Europe to produce a thesis with the unwieldy title of *Appeasement at Munich: The Inevitable Result of the Slowness of the British Democracy to Change From a Disarmament Policy*. In a letter to his father Jack wrote, "Just finished my thesis. It was only going to run about the average length, 70 pages, but finally ran to 150 ... it represents more work than I've ever done in my life." The public relations man in Joe Kennedy saw instantly that this unexceptionable paper might be refashioned into a topical book which would establish Jack as a public figure. Reworked by *New York Times* journalist Arthur Krock, crammed with graphs and charts supplied by the ambassador, and with a foreword by Henry Luce, Jack's paper was relaunched as *Why England Slept* and published in the summer of 1940. Its entry into the best-seller lists was helped by the ambassador who bought 40,000 copies and stored them at Hyannis Port. The book sold particularly well in the United Kingdom, and autographed copies were sent to the King and Queen. Harold Laski, who was also sent a copy, struck a sour note with the tart observation that "I don't honestly think that any publisher would have looked at that book of Jack's if he had not been your son, and if you had not been the ambassador".

Why England Slept is infused with Jack Kennedy's romantic view of the British character derived from the small, exclusive circles in which he had moved in 1939 and with which he felt a natural affinity. Teasing a conclusion from its clotted argument is difficult – Joe Jr remarked that the book "represented a lot of work but didn't prove anything" – but one of its themes leans heavily on the ambassador's anxiety that the democracies' belated mobilization might force them to put aside the freedom for which they were fighting. Taking a more positive view, Jack called this pheneomenon "voluntary totalitariansim", in which all of the state's energies "would have to be molded in one direction". Some Kennedy biographers have seen in this an embryonic formulation of Jack's exhortation in his inaugural address to "Ask not what your country can do for you, but what you can do for your country".

At the time the ambassador was less concerned with the coherence of Jack's arguments thanthe introduction to the American public of a Promising Young Writer. He wrote to Jack, "You would be surprised how a book that really makes the grade with high-class people stands you in good stead for years to come." Just like a Hollywood studio boss who eases a young actor out of the B-movies and into the limelight, the ambassador was creating a "star" within the family.

In the summer of 1940, the Kennedy family friend Charles Spalding observed the Kennedys in their element and in perpetual motion at Hyannis Port: "Jack was autographing copies of *Why England Slept* while Grandfather Fitzgerald was reading to

Lieutenant Jack Kennedy cutting a jaunty figure in the Pacific. Operations in the PT-boat he commanded were admirably suited to his dashing style, but his weak back took a terrific pounding in the light plywood-hulled craft.

him a political story from a newspaper. Young Joe was telling about something which happened to him in Russia. [Joe Jr had visited the Soviet Union with Harold Laski in the early 1930s and had been briefly impressed by socialism. Later he became as politically conservative as his father and a convinced isolationist.] Mrs Kennedy was on the phone talking to Cardinal Spellman. A tall and very attractive girl in a sweatshirt and dungarees, who turned out to be Pat, was describing how a Messerschmitt plane had crashed near her father's home outside London. Bobby was trying to get everyone to play charades. The next thing I knew all of us were choosing up sides for touch football and Kathleen was calling the plays in the huddle for the team I was on. There was something doing every minute. The conversation at the dinner table was wonderful, lively and entertaining, ranging from the war and Washington politics to books, sports and show business." Soon, however, this idyll was to be shattered by the fortunes of war.

Joe Jr and Jack joined up before the Japanese attacked Pearl Harbor on 7 December 1941. Joe enlisted as a Navy flier, reporting for training at the Squantum Naval Air Facility, near Boston. Jack had idled away a few aimless weeks at Stanford Business School before leaving to build up his strength to pass the Navy's fitness test. In truth, without his father's influence he would never have passed, but the ambassador's "pull" with Captain Alan Kirk, Director of the Office of Naval Intelligence and a former Naval attaché in London, ensured that Jack received only the most cursory of examinations.

Jack was immediately granted a commission as an ensign – something which rankled with Joe Jr, now training to fly Catalina maritime patrol aircraft – and was assigned a desk job with Naval Intelligence in Washington, where he was working at the time of Pearl Harbor.

In Washington Jack fell straight into the arms of Inga Arvad, an attractive twice-married Danish journalist five years older than himself who worked on the *Times-Herald*. "Inga Binga", as Jack called her, was a woman with a past of which he was blithely unaware. In the 1930s she had been on notably friendly terms with many of the Nazi leaders and had also been the mistress of a Swedish journalist with Nazi connections. All this was known to the FBI, who suspected Arvad of being a Nazi spy and had placed her under surveillance. The suspicions were later proved to be groundless, but her lovemaking with her new friend in Naval Intelligence was captured on tape. Eventually the tapes found their way into that black hole of compromising information, the private files of J. Edgar Hoover. Almost certainly this, and other well-documented Kennedy indiscretions, account for the Kennedys' kid-glove handling of the old monster during Jack's presidency. He had the goods on them and they knew it.

Jack Kennedy's dangerous liaison with "Inga Binga" threatened to bring his brief Navy career to an abrupt end. When the Office of Naval Intelligence learned of the affair a court martial was considered, and it was only the ambassador's prominent position which saved Jack. He was banished to Charleston, South Carolina, to teach factory workers the rudiments of civil defense.

In the spring of 1942 his back gave out and he was granted six months inactive duty before signing up for service on PT-boats. At the beginning of the Pacific War, the 80-ft PT-boats – highly maneuverable fast-attack craft – had a special glamor. It had been a PT-boat which had taken General MacArthur off Bataan and for several weeks thereafter they were the only US surface vessels available to fight a delaying action against the rampaging Japanese. However, the popular image of the PT-boats belied their relative ineffectiveness. Their engines and radio equipment were highly unreliable, they were easily detected at night by their phosphorescent wake, and they were liable to explode in a ball of flame at the first direct hit. Nevertheless, they remained an attractive prospect for dashing Ivy League types with sailing experience and a reluctance to work their way slowly up to command in bigger ships.

In March 1943, after six months of training, Lieutenant Jack Kennedy was posted to the South Pacific as a replacement to take command of *PT-109*, part of a squadron which had already seen action in the Solomon

Jack with members of PT-109's crew. From left to right, George "Barney" Ross, JFK, Paul "Red" Fay, a close friend who later served as Under Secretary of the Navy during Jack's presidency, and James "Jim" Reed. Jack commanded PT-109 with a cavalier disregard for regulations, jettisoning the life raft to accommodate a 37mm gun fixed on a plank on the forward deck. However, the plank played an important part in the rescue phase of the PT-109 incident, as did Jack's swimming training at Harvard without which he might not have saved the life of crew member Patrick McMahon.

Islands. Of all the fighting ships on which Jack could have served, the PT-boat was the least suitable. The vibrations which shook the plywood hull took their toll on his unstable back, but the Kennedy drive to be in the thick of the action could not be denied. George Ross, *PT-109*'s third officer, recalled: "He always liked to be first when the boats would have a race in after a patrol ... he was going a little too fast, and the reverse gear failed, and he plowed into the gas dock there on the Russell Islands. How flustered the squadron commander was! Jack could see he was about to get chewed down and he said, 'Well you can't stop that *PT-109*.' That got a lot of laughs."

By August 1943 the tide of Japanese

conquest in the Pacific was in retreat. In two crucial naval battles, Coral Sea (4-8 May 1942) and Midway (4 June 1942) the Japanese had first been halted and then decisively defeated. The recapture of Guadalcanal, which marked the beginning of the Allied reconquest of the Pacific, was completed at the beginning of February 1943. In the Solomons the primary Allied objectives were the islands of Bougainville and New Georgia.

On the night of 1 August *PT-109*'s squadron sailed from its base at Lumbari Island to patrol the Blackett Strait, which separates the island of Vila from New Georgia and through which the Japanese were running heavily escorted convoys, dubbed "The Tokyo Express", to reinforce the garrisons on Vela

Lavella, Vila and the airstrip at Munda on New Georgia. The squadron's task was to intercept and attack "The Tokyo Express" on its way in and out of the Blackett Strait.

PT-109 missed the convoy on its inward journey, taking evasive action after being caught in a destroyer's searchlight. Later that night, which was dark and starless, *PT-109* formed part of a picket line waiting to catch the Japanese on their return journey.

What happened next became the stuff of legend, although the precise facts remain unclear. At about 2.30am on 2 August, while idling with only one of her three engines turning over, *PT-109* was rammed by the Japanese destroyer *Amagiri*. She was sliced in two, her fuel tanks exploded and Kennedy gave the order to abandon ship. Daylight found the survivors of the ramming clinging to part of *PT-109*'s hull. Two of the thirteen-man crew had been lost and a third, Patrick McMahon, was badly wounded. Kennedy had swum out to save him in the immediate aftermath of the explosion. From their exposed position Kennedy and his crew could see the activity in a Japanese camp on the nearby island of Gizo.

Kennedy's subsequent conduct showed a combination of sheer physical courage and impetuosity. That night the survivors paddled behind a plank salvaged from *PT-109* to an island three miles away. Throughout the five-hour swim Kennedy swam breaststroke, pulling McMahon behind him, a strap from the wounded man's Mae West clenched between his teeth. Having reached temporary safety, he

swam out into the strait with a lantern in the hope of attracting a passing PT-boat, a grueling sortie in which he was almost swept away by the strong current. The survivors then made a second long swim to a larger island, Kennedy again towing the helpless McMahon. Another risky expedition by Kennedy, this time accompanied by George Ross, led to the discovery of a Japanese cache of food on a neighboring atoll. But when the two men ventured out over the reef in a native canoe they had found, they nearly came to grief in a squall.

What Kennedy could not know was that, on the morning after the ramming, the wreckage of *PT-109* had been spotted by an Australian coastwatcher, Lieutenant Arthur Reginald Evans, from his secret outpost on the volcanic outcrop of Kolombangara. It was Evans' sighting, and his dispatch of a search party to locate the survivors, which saved Kennedy and his crew, rather than the message Jack scrawled on a coconut when he encountered some of the search party on the fifth day of their ordeal. But the coconut was to loom large in the subsequent celebrations of *PT-109*, and during Jack's presidency it occupied pride of place on his desk in the Oval Office.

On 7 August seven natives in a war canoe arrived to take Kennedy to Evans. Two wire service correspondents were aboard the PT-boats which sailed that night from Lumbari to pick up *PT-109*'s crew. The story made the front page of the New York Times under the headline "Kennedy's Son Saves 10 in Pacific as Destroyer Splits His PT-boat". Much was made

of Jack's coconut message but there was no mention of an earlier message given to the natives by crewman Lennie Thom while Kennedy and Ross were stranded on the neighboring atoll after their adventure with the canoe. Security required silence on Evans' role in the drama.

For public consumption Jack Kennedy was a hero, however within the Navy the *PT-109* affair was considered something of an embarrassment. It was the first and last time in the Pacific war that a PT-boat was run down by a Japanese warship. In retrospect it appears that Kennedy and his crew were, quite literally, caught napping. They had not responded to the frantic signals of another PT-boat on the picket line which saw the *Amagiri* plowing toward her sister-ship.

Jack had displayed courage and endurance during the rescue phase, saving McMahon's life, but his subsequent efforts to raise help were perhaps more foolhardy than practical. Nevertheless, Kennedy's commanding officer recommended him for the Silver Star, a combat medal, the citation incorrectly stating that he had "personally rescued three men"; he had rescued only McMahon in the hours after the sinking.

Nine months later Kennedy was awarded the relatively modest "lifesaving" Navy and Marine Corps medal – a measure of the Navy's misgivings over the ramming and a tribute to the persistence of the ambassador, who had been badgering his friend James Forrestal, the Under-Secretary of the Navy.

Lieutenant Kennedy at the wheel of PT-109.

Had Jack Kennedy not been the ambassador's son, the loss of *PT-109* would have remained a small footnote to the history of the Pacific War. But Joe Kennedy was to extract the maximum mileage from the "official" Kennedy version, which appeared in "Survival", a 1944 New Yorker piece written by John Hersey. In "Survival" *PT-109*'s crew appear on the alert and on the attack: "Kennedy saw a large shape and spun the wheel to attack", a maneuver which would have only presented the Amagiri with an easier target.

Nevertheless, when a heavily edited version of "Survival" appeared in the Reader's Digest, Jack Kennedy was still spinning the wheel to attack, a phrase calculated to cast him in the heroic mold promoted by the ambassador. Later *PT-109* became a potent symbol in Jack's campaigns, and the *PT-109* tie-clip a token of the New Frontier. Fact blended with fiction in Robert Donovan's best-selling account of Jack's Navy career, which not surprisingly makes no mention of Inga Arvad and places Jack in the Pentagon before it was built. The citation with which Kennedy provided Donovan and also another biographer, James MacGregor Burns, was the preliminary and inaccurate draft submitted by his commanding officer, not the final version. By then *PT-109* had assumed a life of its own. A fast attack craft with *PT-109* markings was one of the highlights of Kennedy's inaugural parade, and in the White House Jack supervised every aspect of the feature film, starring Cliff Robertson, which was based on Donovan's book. However, in 1961, shortly after the Bay of Pigs debacle, he had sufficient candor to tell Donovan that the *PT-109* affair was "more fucked-up than Cuba".

The rest of Jack's Navy career was an anticlimax. In December 1943 he returned to the United States with malaria and a recurrence of his back problem. In June 1944 he underwent an unsuccessful and debilitating disk operation. He was discharged by the Navy at the end of 1944 "by reason of physical disability".

By then the Kennedys had been dealt two heavy blows. Jack's return as a war hero had been a bitter pill for Joe Jr to swallow. After the party held to celebrate Jack's homecoming, a guest heard Joe Jr weeping with rage in the next bedroom. Always considered the most dynamic and the one destined for greatness, Joe Jr had been upstaged by his younger brother at every turn since 1940. There had been the best-selling *Why England Slept*, Jack's immediate commission, and now the drama of *PT-109*. For much of the war Joe Jr had been stranded far from the front line in Puerto Rico, flying uneventful anti-submarine patrols. Posted to England and stationed in Cornwall, the monotonous routine continued over the gray waters of the Atlantic. His tour was completed by the mid-summer of 1944, but desperate to retrieve his position of primacy among the Kennedy children, Joe Jr volunteered for the extremely hazardous "Aphrodite" project aimed at destroying the V-weapons installations in the Pas de Calais. For "Aphrodite", battle-weary bombers were stripped out and turned into huge guided missiles containing 20,000 lb of Torpex explosive triggered by an impact fuse system. The pilot took off manually, in an open cockpit, and then bailed out by parachute near the English coast after setting the fuse. A director aircraft then took over the steering of the bomber by radio.

It was almost as if Joe Jr had a death wish. Before the "Aphrodite" mission on 12 August his electronics engineer urged a delay to check the wiring. But Joe Jr pressed on. His converted US Navy Liberator bomber exploded prematurely at 15,000 ft. So terrible was the explosion that blast damage on the ground extended over a radius of six miles.

The ambassador was shattered by his eldest son's death. A month later the Kennedys' grief was compounded when "Billy" Hartington, whom Kathleen had married in the summer, was killed in action in France. Lem Billings recalled that after Joe Jr's death the ambassador "had the look on his face of someone who has seen something frightening and can't get it out of his mind". Never again could he mention Joe Jr without giving way to tears. The hopes which he had nursed for Joe Jr, who was to live out the political triumphs which had eluded his father, were now transferred to Jack. Resigned to his fate, Jack told his Navy friend, Paul "Red" Fay, "I'm it now, you know. It's my turn. I've got to perform."

Lieutenant Kennedy receives his Navy and Marine Corps medal, 12 June 1944.

Chapter Three

Young Man in a Hurry

JFK wooing skeptical voters in Boston harbor in his 1946 campaign for Congress. The fedora he was so reluctant to wear throughout the campaign remains in his hand. Although a big fedora was the trademark of a Boston politician in the late 1940s, Jack hated wearing a hat, believing, with some justification, that it removed half of the character from his face.

At first Jack was reluctant to step into the breach left by Joe Jr's death. While slowly recovering his health, he tried his hand at journalism, covering the Potsdam conference and the United Nations conference at San Francisco for Hearst Newspapers. Hearst also sent him to Britain to cover the General Election of July 1945, in which Winston Churchill was turned out of office by a Labour Party landslide. A lingering Kennedy myth suggests that Jack predicted the Labour victory, but there is no evidence to confirm this. Jack was only playing at journalism and Arthur Krock provides a fleeting glimpse of the future, relaxed Kennedy style at the San Francisco conference, where he mingled with the great and the good and enjoyed himself mightily. Krock spotted Kennedy lolling on a hotel bed in full evening dress, cocktail in one hand and telephone receiver in the other, leaving a languid message for his editor, "Tell him that Kennedy will not be filing tonight." Jack also visited the Hollywood fleshpots, renewing his acquaintaince with old flame Inga Arvad and romancing the beautiful actress Gene Tierney. Like his father, Jack had an almost naive fascination with the Hollywood dream factory. The power of the image-makers excited him, as did inside knowledge, the gossip and scandal which ran through Hollywood, the dark side of the American Dream. Jack was – and would always remain – starstruck. The principal reasons behind Jack's subsequent compromising friendship with Frank Sinatra

were the singer's access to starlets and his fund of salacious stories about Tinseltown's finest.

While Jack enjoyed himself in Hollywood, the ambassador continued to mourn Joe Jr with a combination of pathetic resignation and bitterness. Shortly before Roosevelt secured his fourth term Joe Kennedy greeted vice-presidential candidate Harry Truman with the words, "Harry, what are you doing campaigning for that crippled son of a bitch that killed my son Joe?"

Characteristically, the ambassador consoled himself with the consolidation of his fortune. During the war he had turned to real estate, acquiring tracts of property in mid-Manhattan and elsewhere and selling them on at a huge profit. His crowning deal was the purchase for $13 million in 1945 of the Merchandise Mart in Chicago, then the largest office building in the world. Joe Kennedy was now one of the few men in America who could write a cheque for $10 million without having to sell something first.

Meanwhile he was quietly clearing the way for Jack's entry into politics. He sold the liquor importing business and eschewed some lucrative but potentially embarrassing ventures into the defense industry. He re-established the connections he had severed with Massachusetts in 1926 with some discreetly publicized acts of charity; and the seat which he filled on a committee reporting on the state's postwar economy enabled him to make a thorough reconnaissance of the political ground.

Boston had proved too small for Joe Kennedy's social and financial ambitions but now it was to provide the launching pad for Jack's political career. Jack knew there was little point in resistance. During his long convalescence after leaving the Navy he had joked with a friend that the frozen steaks and books which the ambassador was sending him were his father's way of ensuring that he was "fattened up in body and mind" for the challenges which lay ahead. He was also aware that, for the moment, he must live Joe Jr's life as well as his own. For the ironic, detached Jack, living in Joe Jr's shadow had its compensations, giving a freedom of maneuver which he was now about to lose. Now he, rather than Joe, was the lightning conductor for his father's fierce ambitions. But he was still running a race with his brother that he could never win. Joe's death had frozen him forever in the attitude of the family's lost leader, and it was toward his dead son that the ambassador's innermost yearnings were still directed. Symbolically, in the closing months of the war the ambassador had used his influence with James Forrestal to name a new destroyer the USS Joseph P. Kennedy Jr, and it was on this ship that Bobby later sailed briefly on his military service. Three months after the launching of the destroyer the ambassador won his persistent battle to declassify the facts of Joe Jr's last mission and secure their release to the public. Jack remarked ruefully to Lem Billings, "I'm shadow boxing in a match the shadow is

JFK on the stump in his first political campaign in 1946. Initially a hesitant public speaker, he was nevertheless quick on his feet when heckled, and was blessed with an "aggressive shyness" which women voters found particularly appealing.

always going to win." He would have to find himself before he could lay his brother's ghost to rest.

The battleground which the ambassador chose was the Massachusetts congressional district vacated by the legendary Boston "pol" James Michael Curley, whose career was celebrated in Edwin O'Connor's novel The Last Hurrah and who was running for Mayor for the fourth time. Jack had already been eased into the world of Boston politics, adopting an official address at the Bellevue Hotel, where "Honey Fitz" lived in retirement, and undertaking a series of informal speaking engagements, coordinated by a public relations agency, in which he talked about his war career and experiences as a journalist.

On the face of it, Jack was ill suited to campaigning in the political rough and tumble of Boston. He was so thin his suits seemed several sizes too big for his wasted frame. With unconscious irony a Hyannis Port Rotarian called Jack "a little boy dressed up in his father's clothes". Drawn, diffident and a desperately hesitant public speaker, Jack was ill at ease in the colorful company of veteran "pols" who could still remember "Honey Fitz" belting out his signature tune Sweet Adeline while on the stump. Gladhanding street corner politics did not come naturally to Jack, nor the famous "Fitzblarney" of his maternal grandfather, who could carry on several conversations at once, amid a throng of supporters. Tip O'Neill, then a member of the state legislature, met Jack for the first time just before St Patrick's Day in 1946. In his memoirs he wrote, "I couldn't believe this skinny, pasty-looking kid was a candidate for *anything*." But the ambassador already had his eyes fixed on the distant political horizon. He told a skeptical local politician, "My son will be President in 1960."

Jack was still a reluctant politician. Frequently in excruciating pain from his back, he had to force himself to press the flesh. One Boston politician recalled, "He was very retiring. You had to lead him by the hand. You had to push him into poolrooms, taverns, clubs and organizations. He didn't like it at first. He wanted no part of it." At one point in the campaign, exhausted and depressed, Jack told some of the Kennedy workers, "I'm just filling Joe's shoes. If he was alive, I'd never be in this."

Jack bobbed unhappily in the sentimental backwash of Irish local politicians. He was reluctant to wear a hat, one of the big gray fedoras which were the traditional distinguishing symbol of the Irish "pol". In this he remained coolly his own man, providing a hint of the detached calculation which would distinguish his method as a mature politician. As Garry Wills wrote, "He had not come to join the Irish pols and certainly not to look like them. He just wanted their votes."

At the beginning of the campaign few observers gave Jack much of a chance. He had several strong opponents in the Democratic primary, including Mike Neville, a popular

Jack leads the Bunker Hill Day parade on the day before the primary vote in 1946. Maximum political advantage was gained from this non-political occasion. Jack took the parade past a veterans' post, named after his brother, of which he was the commander. Retaining his jacket to distinguish him from the column, carefully drawn up three abreast, he received bunches of flowers from a succession of strategically placed young girls, handing them on to women in the crowd. It was a hot day, and after the five-mile walk he collapsed with exhaustion. By the evening, however, he was back in action again.

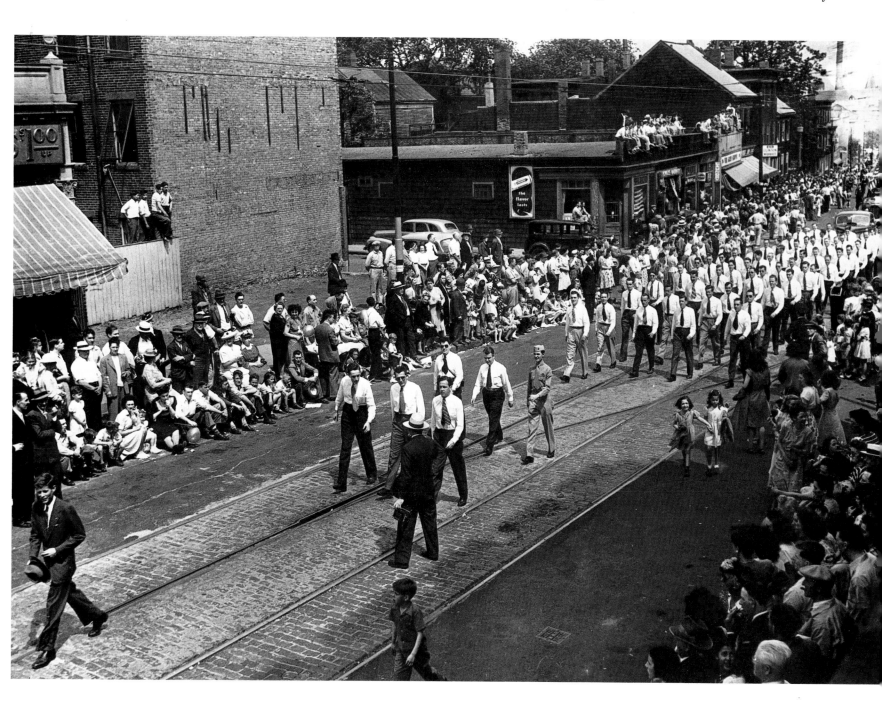

mayor of Cambridge. Tip O' Neill was one of many who wrote off Jack as "a carpetbagger whose father lived in Palm Beach".

They had not reckoned on Kennedy organization and drive, or the ambassador's money. On the ground, Jack's campaign was masterminded by the 66-year-old Joe Kane, a distant relation of the Kennedys and an immensely experienced political operator. He devised the campaign slogan, "The New Generation Offers a Leader", gathered around Jack a team of energetic young war veterans, including Torbert Macdonald, Paul "Red" Fay, Dave Powers and Mark Dalton, and played hard on the candidate's heroism in the South Pacific, flooding the district with copies of the *Reader's Digest* article on *PT-109*. "Honey Fitz" and his cronies were kept well out of the way; "Get that son of a bitch out of here!" bawled Kane when Jack's grandfather turned up at the campaign headquarters.

Behind the scenes the ambassador pulled the strings and disbursed the money, at least $300,000 of it. Tip O'Neill recalled: "A few weeks before the primary, the Kennedys approached a number of large families and promised them $50 in cash to help out at the polls. They didn't really care if these people showed up to work. They were simply buying votes, a few at a time, and fifty bucks was a lot of money. The Kennedys also put on dozens of cocktail parties and teas. If you agreed to invite a few friends to your house to meet Jack, they brought in a case of mixed booze, hired a caterer, and gave you $100 – which

was supposed to pay for a cleaning woman to come to your house before and after the party. If they could convince a large family with six or eight voters to host the event, so much the better."

Some local wags took to carrying a $20 bill in their lapels, referring to it as "a Kennedy campaign button". *The Boston Globe*, a Hearst paper to which the ambassador had extended a large tactical loan, ceased to carry stories about Mike Neville in the weeks leading up to the primary and declined to carry his advertisements. The threat posed by another candidate, Joseph Russo, was dealt with by hiring a man with the same name to run and split the vote.

Mark Dalton remembered the aura of raw power which filled the ambassador's suite at Boston's Ritz Hotel where, flanked by former Police Commissioner Joe Timilty and Archbishop Cushing, the powers temporal and spiritual, he ran the campaign: "It was strong stuff for a young Catholic man like myself. Going to see Mr Kennedy in those days was like going to visit God."

Meanwhile the candidate drove himself on. His politics were unexceptionable, focusing on veterans' housing, a strong military program, the extension of social security benefits, a rise in the minimum wage, and limited reforms of Congress. He spoke out against Communism, Fascism and Socialism. Like the preacher asked about sin, Jack was "agin them". A feature in a local magazine, part of the media campaign orchestrated by the ambassador,

Above: Rose Kennedy keeps a watchful maternal eye on Jack. Opposite: Rose was a tireless campaigner for her son in his 1952 campaign against Henry Cabot Lodge. Occasionally her exuberant endorsements of Jack caused him a frisson of embarrassment. He seems a little bashful here as she warms to her task.

described Jack as a "fighting conservative".

Jack was a wooden speaker but, under pressure, he displayed flashes of an engaging charm which Dave Powers characterized as "aggressive shyness". Struggling toward the end of a speech to a gathering of Gold Star Mothers, women who had lost sons in the war, he won them over with the unaffected declaration, "I think I know how you mothers feel, because my mother is a Gold Star Mother, too."

Women readily responded to his frail good looks. "Red" Fay recalled: "People – particularly the young girls in the junior colleges – would just go wild. He had magnetism."

And he had the Kennedy family working for him. Eunice and Pat attended block parties and campaigned house to house. Bobby was assigned to Lem Billings, covering three working-class wards in Cambridge and throwing himself into the campaign "as if his life and Jack's life depended on it".

Impressive as individuals, the Kennedy family also represented more than the sum of its parts. At the climax of the campaign all the women of the Eleventh District who were registered Democrats were sent engraved invitations to a tea with the family at a hotel in Cambridge. This was the cause of much ribaldry among the "pols", but when the day of the reception fell, 2,000 women queued to get in, many of them wearing rented evening dresses. It was a dramatic early demonstration of the public's eagerness to touch a little of the Kennedy magic.

On 18 June Jack won the primary at a canter, taking 42 per cent of the poll and outpolling his nearest rival, Mike Neville, by two to one. The ambassador made sure that Jack's victory received headline treatment in the New York Times and was treated to a lengthy analysis in the National Affairs section of Time magazine. Time described Jack as "a boyish looking bachelor of twenty-nine" who had "worked to prove that he was no snob".

The autumn election was a shoo-in for Jack, although the rest of Massachusetts saw heavy Republican gains. In the wake of Jack's victory the ambassador established the Joseph P. Kennedy Jr Foundation, president John Fitzgerald Kennedy, through which Archbishop Cushing received $650,000 for a Boston hospital for handicapped children. Jack was still boxing with his brother's shadow.

The publicity fanned by the ambassador followed Jack to Congress, where he arrived in January 1947, having been voted one of the Ten Outstanding Men of 1946 by the US Junior Chamber of Commerce. However, his own career as a congressman was somewhat less than outstanding. His record was distinguished more by absenteeism than by concrete achievement. Tip O'Neill remembered, "In all my public life, I've never seen a congressman get so much press for so little work." But then not every congressman had a father like the ambassador.

Initially Jack cut rather a forlorn figure, living in bachelor chaos in Georgetown and attending the House in rumpled, unmatched jackets and trousers. He had not the slightest idea about money, rarely carried any, and spent much of his time mooching small amounts from friends and colleagues who were seldom repaid. On several occasions he was mistaken for a lift boy. He was still trying to orientate himself in the clearing in the political jungle which had been so ruthlessly hacked for him by his father.

Jack's relentless womanizing at this time owed something to his father's example but also represented an attempt to stake out some ground of his own and to exert an element of control over the "physical disequilibrium" which plagued him. Tip O'Neill wrote that Jack "had more fancy young girls flying in from all over the country than anyone could count". But there seems something joyless in these instant couplings, as if they served only to blot out Jack's pain.

Jack remained a political lightweight, surrounded by a gaggle of cronies-cum-gofers like Billy Sutton and Ted Reardon, with whom he would while away the afternoons in his office tossing a football back and forth. The reward for their loyalty was "the pleasure of his company", although some observers felt they detected an element of casual tyranny underlying the apparently relaxed surface of these relationships.

Jack's politics were liberal on bread-and-butter issues like social security, education, wages and hours regulations, but he followed his father's fiscal conservatism and shared with his constituents a suspicion of big government and a hard-line anti-Communism. In 1950 he told the Harvard Graduate School of Public Affairs that Senator Joe McCarthy, who was beginning to sniff out "Reds" in high places, "may have something". Serving on the House Education and Labor Committee, he attracted nationwide attention with his stern cross-examination of two union officials, Harold Christoffel and Louis Budenz, during an investigation into possible Communist influence behind a 1941 strike at Allis-Chambers in Milwaukee.

Jack became friendly with a "dapper-looking" young Republican congressman serving on the Committee, Richard M. Nixon, to whose 1950 campaign for the US Senate against the liberal Helen Gahagan Douglas the ambassador was to contribute $50,000. Jack felt comfortable in the company of conservatives and was also on good terms with the Republican Joe McCarthy, who was a friend of the ambassador and had dated two of the Kennedy girls.

Casting a cloud over Jack's political future was the continuing frailty of his health. In 1947, while on a Congressional fact-finding tour of Europe, he fell seriously ill in London. He was diagnosed to be suffering from Addison's disease, a rare life-threatening deficiency in the production of hormones by the cortex and the adrenal glands. One of Jack's friends, Pamela Churchill, was told by a doctor that, in his opinion, Jack had less than a year to live.

Jack sailed home on the Queen Mary and was administered extreme unction by a priest the moment the liner docked in New York.

His condition was brought under control with a synthetic substance, DOCA, which adjusted the hormonal imbalance. Rather than subject Jack to a regime of constant injections, pellets of DOCA were implanted in his thighs every three months. About a couple of years later he began taking oral doses of the newly developed hormone, cortisone, which enabled him to live a relatively normal life. As a precautionary measure, Joe Kennedy stashed supplies of DOCA and cortisone in safe deposit boxes all over the United States.

In the Kennedy creed, weakness could not be tolerated. From his childhood Jack had been chronically ailing, but this could not be admitted, either within the family or to the public. The unstable back from which he had suffered since boyhood was explained away as being caused by the strain he suffered while rescuing his comrades after the sinking of *PT-109*. The weight loss and yellowish complexion associated with Addison's disease were brushed aside as symptoms of recurrent malaria, again from wartime service, and disguised by Jack with constant sunbathing.

The family's repeated evasions about Jack's multiple health problems eventually led to some economy with the truth when in 1960, during the race for the Democratic presidential nomination, Jack's chief rival Lyndon Johnson leaked a story to the press that his opponent was suffering from Addison's disease. The Kennedy camp issued what amounted to a denial, later rationalizing their response on the grounds that it was justified by the public's misapprehension that the disease was invariably fatal. As it was not, they could deny that Jack was suffering from it.

More remarkable, however, was Jack Kennedy's refusal to submit to the assorted disabilities which afflicted him. After each blow, many of which would have permanently felled a man without such extraordinary reserves of willpower – the "raw guts" which Kennedys prized above all else – Jack got up to meet a new challenge. He had for so long courted physical dangers to forget about his illness that the illness itself became another risk with which to joust.

Death never seemed far away, and in May 1948 it claimed Kathleen. She was killed in a plane crash in France while traveling with Peter, the eighth Earl of Fitzwilliam, whom she intended to marry; Fitzwilliam was also killed in the accident. "Kick" was buried in the Cavendish's family plot at Chatsworth. Joe came to the funeral, griefstricken and out of place among "Kick's" aristocratic British friends. Rose, who had refused to countenance the marriage – Fitzwilliam was a playboy, a Protestant, and already married – stayed away.

Kathleen's death had a profound effect on Jack, plunging him into a long period of introspection in which he cornered close friends like Congressman George Smathers and discussed with them the best way to die. He found a new role model, Lord Byron, whose physical disability (a club foot) and legendary power over women stimulated Jack's seemingly insatiable appetite for sex. When he was challenged by a female acquaintance over the risk of scandalous exposure that he was running, Jack could only reply wistfully, "I guess I can't help it."

Tip O'Neill thought that Jack Kennedy was "like a fish out of water" in Congress. Later Jack considered that he and his fellow congressmen "were like worms over there". Eugene McCarthy, then a congressman from Minnesota, recalled an incident during Jack's second term when he watched Kennedy stroll on to the floor of the House and say to himself, "Well, if you don't want to work for a living, this is as good a job as any."

There was an absence of political passion in his life. In a 1952 television interview he said, "I think that's the difficulty in politics. You are always bound to lose supporters once you have taken a stand on an issue."

Long before this Jack and the ambassador had determined to "go statewide" in Massachusetts, although which office Jack would seek remained undecided. Shortly after his second re-election to Congress, Jack set about raising his profile, making a series of sweeps through Massachusetts, addressing meetings and shaking hands. To establish a reputation as an expert on foreign affairs, he traveled to the Middle and Far East in 1951, accompanied by Eunice and Bobby. It was on this fact-finding tour that the two brothers, separated by eight years, got to know each

A face at the back of the crowd: the youthful profile of Congressman Kennedy can be glimpsed on an official occasion during his 1951 visit to Vietnam.

Left: Congressman Kennedy indicates some potential Third World flashpoints. In the 1950s he maintained a consistent interest in the problems thrown up by the withdrawal of the colonial powers, particularly in the Far East. In the early 1960s there were few American politicians better qualified to deal with the crises in Laos and Vietnam. Opposite: With Bobby in the 1952 campaign.

other well and laid the foundations of a powerful political partnership. As a child Bobby had fought hard to establish his place in the Kennedy pecking order. Awkward, inarticulate and lacking the charm which eased Jack's passage, he had won respect and academic honors by sheer willpower. The intensity which had sustained him as he grew up, and which radiated from his hawklike features, was to be translated with great effect into his political life.

French Indochina was on the Kennedys' itinerary. At Saigon Congressman Kennedy was met by an impressive array of high-ranking French officers, bursting to brief him on the progress of the war against the Communist Viet Minh and eager to introduce him to handpicked Vietnamese officers, sleek in their paratroop uniforms and living proof, they claimed, of the Vietnamese Army's steadfast determination to defeat the Communist guerrillas.

The encounter was an eerie preview of the 1960s, but the skeptical young congressman obtained an entirely different perspective from journalists on the spot, who painted a gloomy picture of the progress of the war. He was told that, far from defeating the Viet Minh, the French were giving ground. A disaffected young foreign service officer, Edmund A. Gullion, explained that the most potent force against the French was not Communism but nationalism. At night from his room at the US embassy, Jack could see the flash of the Viet Minh guns which ringed Saigon. Intuitively he realized that there was no future for French colonialism in Vietnam.

In Japan Jack fell dangerously ill again. His temperature rose to 106° F and the doctors attending him feared for his life. He rallied, and on his return to the United States gave a radio talk on the trip in which he asserted that "the fires of nationalism so long dormant have been kindled and are now ablaze", adding that "Communism cannot be met by force of arms".

In 1952 Jack ran for the Senate against the heavily entrenched incumbent Henry Cabot Lodge Jr. The contest was ripe with irony, as it had been Lodge's grandfather who had beaten "Honey Fitz" in 1916. A polished, liberal Republican, Lodge was the embodiment of the Brahmin culture which the ambassador so despised. Compared with the Cabots and the Lodges, who talked only to each other and to God, the Kennedys were an upstart dynasty.

Confident of victory, Lodge passed a message to Joe Kennedy that he was wasting his money. He would crush Jack by 300,000 votes, just as he had a popular Democratic challenger in 1946. Once again their opponents had underestimated the Kennedys' will to win. They had already prepared the ground in a demonstration of the method which Henry Fairlie later called "the Kennedy campaign before the campaign". Francis X. Morrissey, Jack's executive assistant in Massachusetts, recalled the series of statewide sweeps Jack had made in his years as a congressman: "In four and a half years we never took more than ten minutes to eat. We lived on cheeseburgers, hamburgers, malted milks and 'frappes' – milk shakes with ice cream in them. By Election Day 1952, we had been in 351 cities and towns, and appeared many times in each. I'll bet he talked to at least a million people and shook hands with 750,000."

It was in 1952 that the "Kennedy machine" took shape. In 1946 Jack's team had been staffed by wartime friends who were now pursuing their own careers. These enthusiastic amateurs were replaced by professionals who approached politics as a science rather than an art: the young Merchandise Mart executive R. Sargent Shriver, who was to become the most honorary of "honorary Kennedys" when he married Eunice in 1953; Kenny O'Donnell, a tough Harvard-educated friend of Bobby; Larry O'Brien, a smart political operator with contacts all over Massachusetts; and to add some gravitas and woo the Cambridge intellectuals, James Landis, former dean of

Opposite:Jack fought the 1952 campaign against Henry Cabot Lodge in almost constant pain, and it was not always possible to screen his physical infirmities from the public. Here he resorts to crutches during one of the Kennedys' famous "tea parties". Even when lame, he was a tough campaigner. Dave Powers recalled, "As long as there was a vote to get, he kept going."

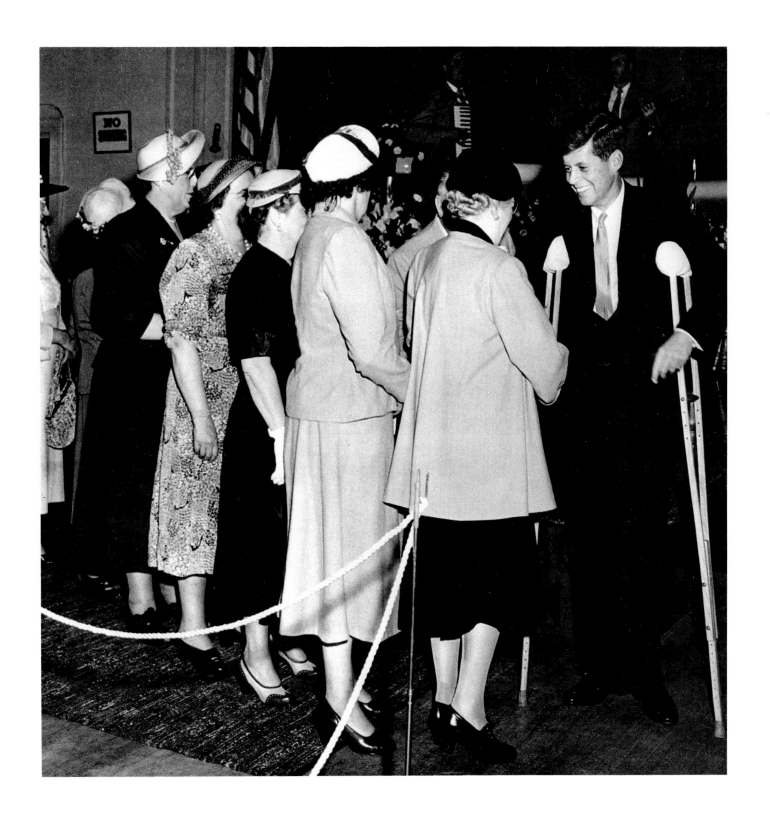

Right: The 1952 campaign saw Jack's first encounters with television. Here Eunice Kennedy models a topical outfit, decorated with the Democratic Party donkey, on "Coffee With the Kennedys", an informal phone-in program. Opposite: Jack surrounded by female admirers at a "tea party".

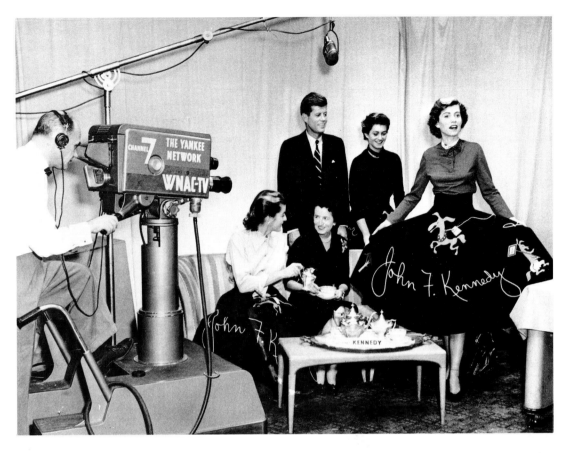

Harvard Law School and veteran New Dealer, who had advised Jack in his Congress days. O'Brien and O'Donnell set up a statewide network of 281 committee secretaries who could deploy over 50,000 full- and part-time volunteers, many of them so young that the word went out that the Kennedy campaign was "in the hands of boys and girls". But it was his appeal to the young which was a powerful political weapon, not least in the presidential election of 1960.

None of this could have been achieved without the controlling financial hand and strategic direction of the ambassador. He bought the support of the initially hostile Boston Post by loaning its editor $500,000 and

it was Kennedy money which paid for the blizzard of posters and reprints of the *Reader's Digest* article on *PT-109*, and also exploited to the hilt the relatively new medium of television.

When Lodge sought the active support of Joe McCarthy, then at the height of his popularity, the ambassador purchased the senator's neutrality with a substantial contribution to his own election campaign. The ambassador also persuaded the liberal Democratic presidential candidate of 1952, Adlai Stevenson, to refrain from making any anti-McCarthy speeches while campaigning in Massachusetts, anticipating that an attack from this quarter would only rebound on

Jack. When another member of the Kennedy team, the liberal Pat Jackson, produced a Kennedy poster which bore the slogan "Communism and McCarthyism: Both Wrong", the ambassador, furious and foul-mouthed, moved instantly to withdraw it. Throughout the campaign, Jack avoided any direct references to the Red-baiting senator and Kennedy family friend.

While Joe fixed the big names, Bobby rode ramrod on the day-to-day campaigning, acting as Jack's hatchet-man with a relish which was later to earn him the nickname of "The Black Prince". When some bruised aides complained to Jack he replied testily, "... everybody bitches about Bobby, and I'm getting sick and goddam tired of it. He's the only one who doesn't stick knives in my back, the only one I can count on when it comes down to it."

The final nail in Lodge's political coffin was the tea and coffee party blitz presided over by the Kennedy women. Tens of thousands of women lined up to meet the candidate and his family – at the first reception nearly 8,000 queued outside a hotel which could hold only 400. The candidate was the main attraction. Outside one Kennedy event, a Republican watching young female Kennedy volunteers moving through the crowd distributing campaign literature was moved to wonder, "What is there about Kennedy that makes every Catholic girl in Boston between eighteen and twenty-eight think it's a holy crusade to get him elected?" A Kennedy family

friend commented, "Poor old Lodge never had a chance. The Kennedys were like a panzer division mowing down the state." Later, Lodge would reflect ruefully, "It was those damned tea parties."

Riding this tidal wave of enthusiasm, Jack remained careful to conceal his physical infirmities. Throughout the campaign he was in constant pain from his back, which he had badly jarred while sliding down a fire station pole in an ill-advised election stunt. Away from the public gaze, he often had to use crutches. To relieve his back, Jack took frequent hot baths. He found comfort only in water so scalding that Dave Powers could barely put his fist in it. While Jack bathed, he remained the center of intense tactical discussions, nicknamed "tub talks" by his entourage.

Jack had been campaigning for four years. Lodge, who had been preoccupied with masterminding General Eisenhower's bid for the presidency, only began to campaign hard two months before polling day. He never recovered from this belated start. In spite of a massive Eisenhower victory in Massachusetts and a Republican landslide in the State House, Jack Kennedy defeated Lodge by more than 70,000 votes with 51.5 per cent of the vote. On election night, as Jack's victory became clear, Rose Kennedy said, "At last the Fitzgeralds have evened the score with the Lodges." It had cost the ambassador anything up to a million dollars. The ousted governor of Massachusetts, Paul Dever, acknowledging Jack's victory and his enormous charm, hailed

Jack at the moment of victory in the campaign against Henry Cabot Lodge. Kennedy workers provided the tickertape by tearing up piles of campaign literature.

Jack as "the first Irish Brahmin".

When he entered the Senate in January 1953, Jack Kennedy was universally recognized as the most eligible bachelor in the United States. In 1951, at a Washington dinner party, he had met for the first time the woman he was to marry, twenty-three-year-old Jacqueline Bouvier. In the autumn of 1952 they began what Jackie would later describe as "a spasmodic courtship".

The first Bouvier in America was a French cabinetmaker who arrived in 1815 and made a fortune in land speculation. Marriage allied the Bouviers with the Drexels and the House of Morgan. They appeared in the Social Register in 1880, about the time that "PJ" Kennedy was moving from saloonkeeping into politics. By the time Jackie was born in 1929 much of the family wealth had been dissipated by her father John V. Bouvier III, a notorious rake and philanderer popularly known as "Black Jack". Jacqueline's mother Janet had divorced "Black Jack" in 1940 and two years later married Hugh D. Auchincloss, a multimillionaire with impeccable social credentials. Jacqueline and her sister Lee lived with their mother and stepfather, but Jackie's real affections remained with the dissolute and darkly handsome "Black Jack", who was obliged by the stingy Auchincloss to support her from his rapidly dwindling resources.

In her childhood and adolescence Jackie had been given the best of everything, studying at Vassar and the Sorbonne and traveling widely in Europe. She graduated from George Washington University in 1951 and then beat a field of over a thousand to win the Prix de Paris competition held by Vogue magazine. Paris and a career in fashion journalism beckoned, but Jackie stayed in America, fearing that if she went to France, she "would never come back".

Jackie's natural chic and gazelle-like beauty belied the fact that in 1952 she had no money of her own and was living off the $42.50 a week she earned as the "enquiring photographer" for the Washington Times Herald – a job she had secured with the help of Arthur Krock, who was a friend of her stepfather. Curiously, her predecessors in the post had included Inga Arvad and Jack's sister Kathleen.

Jackie was very different proposition to the nameless young women who had shuttled in and out of Jack's Georgetown home in his days as a congressman. Behind the wide-apart eyes, soft voice and wistful smile was an independent young woman with a cultured intelligence, barbed wit and a mind which her private secretary later likened to a steel trap. Her pleasures were often solitary; reading and listening to music. Jack was drawn by her detachment and esthetic interests, but these qualities did not endear Jackie to the Kennedy women, with whom she spent much of her engagement in a state of undeclared war. After breaking an ankle in a scrimmage on the lawn at Hyannis Port, Jackie withdrew from the pell-mell of touch football and was the butt of much strident ragging from Jack's sisters, who

Jack and Jackie enjoy a quiet moment together at Hyannis Port. Jackie later wrote of Jack's courtship,"He was not the candy-and-flowers type, so every now and then he'd give me a book. He gave me The Raven, *which is the life of Sam Houston, and also* Pilgrim's Way.*"*

dubbed her "The Debutante" and teased her mercilessly about her little-girl voice and unusually large feet.

In contrast, she got on famously with the ambassador, as dominating a father figure as her own adored "Black Jack" and as cynical in his treatment of women.

In January 1953, at Eisenhower's inaugural ball, Lem Billings warned Jackie about Jack's womanizing and the unlikelihood of it stopping if she decided to marry him. She took this advice less calmly, seeming to welcome the challenge. Charles Spalding later observed, "She wasn't sexually attracted to men unless they were dangerous like old 'Black Jack'." In May 1953, while Jackie was in England preparing to photograph the coronation of Queen Elizabeth II, Jack Kennedy proposed to her by cable.

They were married at St Mary's Roman Catholic Church in Newport, Rhode Island, on 12 September 1953. The bridegroom's face was heavily scratched from a strenuous early-morning touch football session. "Black Jack" was too drunk to attend the ceremony, but his presence would hardly have been noticed in the throng of 800 guests, among them the entire Senate. The ambassador spared no expense to make the wedding the social event of the year, but the oceans of champagne he provided did not entirely submerge his native vulgarity and the clannishness of the Kennedys.

Jackie did much to domesticate Jack, subtly working on his careless dress and offhand manners. In public she played the dutiful wife to perfection, a beautiful presence hovering behind the young senator, while he read "I Have a Rendezvous with Death" on Edward R. Murrow's television show Person to Person, and the charming subject of the frequent photo-opportunities the Kennedys granted an eager press. But like her mother-in-law she had to reconcile herself to her husband's infidelities.

The year of Jack's marriage to Jacqueline Bouvier also saw his political marriage to Theodore Sorensen, a brilliant, ambitious twenty-four-year-old Nebraskan attorney with a family background of untrammeled liberalism which contrasted sharply with the conservatism of the Kennedys. After two short interviews Jack engaged Ted Sorensen as his legislative assistant.

It was a momentous decision. Sorensen was the first important aide who was Jack's choice rather than his father's, and the first to come from outside the closed world of the Kennedys. And it was Sorensen who gave Jack his distinctive political voice. As his speechwriter he drew out of Jack a wit and oratorical richness which had previously only intermittently graced his political vocabulary. Additionally, the stream of crisp, well-informed articles which began appearing under Kennedy's name were the product of Sorensen's literary cottage industry.

Like many good partnerships, Kennedy and Sorensen were a combination of opposites. Jack's political career had prospered on his

Previous spread, left: JFK and Jackie, radiantly happy on their wedding day. Right: Jackie with Kennedy menfolk and "honorary Kennedys". Front row, left to right: Hugh G. Auchincloss Jr, Senator George Smathers, Torbert Macdonald, Benjamin Smith. Middle row: Edward Kennedy, Jackie, JFK, Robert Kennedy, James Reed. Back row: Michael Canfield, Charles Bartlett, Paul B. Fay Jr, Lem Billings, Joseph Gargan, R.Sargent Shriver, Charles Spalding.

charm while others had tackled the details. Sorensen, on the other hand, was considered a cold fish by his colleagues, but he had intellectual discipline, a capacity for sustained hard work and command of a ripe, rolling prose style ideally suited to the cadences of Jack's voice. Above all, he was completely loyal, content to supply bullets for the junior senator to fire. Jack called Sorensen "my intellectual blood bank". Another medical analogy would have been equally appropriate. Just as the cortisone Jack took began to fill out his face and frame, lending him an almost irresistible attractiveness as a mature man, so Sorensen's speeches and articles enabled him to expand his intellectual and political profile to an extent which he could never have managed without the transfusion of his aide's particular gifts. They both needed each other and merged their very different political personalities so effectively that, as Sorensen later wrote, "as the years went on, and I came to know what he thought on each subject as well as how he wished to say it, our style and standard became increasingly one". It was not long before Sorensen could imitate Kennedy's voice so effectively that he sometimes impersonated him on the telephone when Jack was too busy to take the call.

Sorensen was drawn to the domestic issues which have traditionally preoccupied liberals. Early in their association Jack asked him what cabinet posts he would choose if he had the pick. Sorensen replied, "Justice, Labor and Health, Education and Welfare." Kennedy dismissed these, opting only for "Secretary of State of Defense". This was, he felt, where the real power lay.

Since his 1951 visit to the Far East, Jack had been focusing much of his attention to the intertwined problems posed by Third World nationalism, the collapse of colonialism and the Communist threat. He saw the end of empire as the preliminary to a new conflict between East and West in which the United States was "the last hope on earth" against the steady spread of Communism. In Vietnam this apocalyptic vision was translated into his advocacy of an indigenous middle way between continuing French rule, financed by the United States, and the Communist Viet Minh. He opposed the Eisenhower administration's request for $400 million of military aid to France, unless the money was used to "encourage through all means available" the freedom and independence Jack believed was desired by the people of Vietnam.

He was an early proponent of the "domino theory" attributed to Eisenhower's Secretary of State John Foster Dulles, arguing – even before Dulles publicly legitimized the theory – that if Vietnam was lost to the Communists, then other countries in the region would topple one by one (Laos, Cambodia, Thailand, Malaya, perhaps even India) as each success gave the insurgents added encouragement and bases to accomplish the next phase. But he differed sharply from the administration over the means by which Communist aggression could be deterred. Kennedy saw that the doctrine of "massive retaliation" – an instant and overwhelming nuclear attack on the Soviet Union or China in response to local conventional involvement – was fast being negated by the growing Soviet nuclear arsenal and was also inappropriate to deal with the increasing number of regional "brush wars" through which the Communists hoped to extend their influence and for which a more flexible counter had to be found.

Kennedy concluded that French colonialism in Vietnam was doomed and that costly attempts to shore it up were equally futile. In the spring of 1954, after suffering a humiliating military defeat at Dien Bien Phu, the French were brought to the conference table at Geneva. On 6 April, three weeks before the conference began, Kennedy made a major speech on the floor of the Senate in which he savaged two years of unrealistically optimistic assessments of the progress of the war, urging that "to pour money, materiel and men into the jungles of Indochina without at least a remote prospect of victory would be dangerously futile and self-destructive ... I am frankly of the belief that no amount of military assistance in Indochina can conquer an enemy that is everywhere and at the same time nowhere."

Following the Geneva conference, Vietnam was divided between North and South along the 17th parallel. The French had been removed from the board but the war continued. Vietnam would return to haunt the Kennedy administration.

At the same time Jack's back problems returned torment him and prompt unwelcome press curiosity about the state of his health. He insisted on undergoing an extremely risky double fusion operation on his back, a procedure complicated by his Addison's disease. He told Larry O'Brien, "this is the one that kills you or cures". It nearly killed him. Following the operation on 21 October Jack slid into a coma and hovered near death. The last rites were administered, but he pulled through and entered a lengthy convalescence.

The operation and the slow, painful period of recuperation (which included a second operation in February 1955) removed Jack from the major domestic political drama of the mid-1950s, the censure of Joe McCarthy by the Senate. McCarthy's reckless and destructive pursuit of Communists in public life had finally been halted during the televised hearings which his Permanent Subcommittee on Investigations had been conducting into the US Army. As a result of the damage that McCarthy inflicted on himself in front of millions of viewers, his enemies in the Senate were finally emboldened to move against him. At the beginning of August 1954 a select committee – handpicked by Majority Leader Lyndon Johnson to leave nothing to chance – was set up to study the matter of McCarthy's censure and to report after the autumn elections.

Jack Kennedy remained ambivalent about McCarthy. As an unreconstructed isolationist,

the ambassador was one of McCarthy's natural constituents and he had long been a friend and strong supporter of the Senator, dismissing as "bunk" allegations that McCarthy's unbridled conduct was doing irreparable damage to the United States' reputation abroad. Moreover, it had been the ambassador who had obtained for Bobby Kennedy the post of minority counsel on McCarthy's committee.

Jack himself was a firm believer in the Red menace. As a congressman he had fired some of the opening shots in the war against domestic subversion and in 1954 he had been one of the prominent backers of the Communist Control Act, which virtually outlawed the Communist Party in the United States. To keep liberal critics at bay, he ventured mild criticisms of McCarthy on points of detail but he hung back from outright condemnation. Recognizing the awkwardness of his position, and the possibility of a censure debate, he had Ted Sorensen prepare a speech for him. But even this only launched an oblique attack on McCarthy by focusing on the misconduct of McCarthy's disagreeable henchman Roy Cohn and Cohn's assistant David Schine, with both of whom Bobby had fallen out violently over the course of the Army-McCarthy hearings. There was no hint of criticism of McCarthy in the speech, never delivered, which confirmed that "Many times I have voted with Senator McCarthy for the full appropriation of funds for his committee, for his amendment to reduce our assistance to nations trading with the Communists, and other matters. I have not

Senator John F. Kennedy at work in his office
on Capitol Hill in 1955.

sought to end his investigations of Communist subversion, nor is the pending measure related to either the desirability or continuation of these investigations."

When the vote to censure McCarthy was passed on 12 December 1954, Jack Kennedy was the only Democrat who failed either to vote or to "pair". Jack's physical incapacity was the reason given for his failure to do so, but at the time the vote was taken he was sufficiently recovered from the first operation to make his position clear from his hospital bed. Later Charles Spalding frankly admitted, "Well, what could he do? He ducked the vote ... All he could think of was he was going to avoid it by not saying anything." Jack waited until the summer of 1956, just a few weeks before the Democratic National Convention, before publicly endorsing McCarthy's censure.

There was still something of the Choate schoolboy in Jack Kennedy. His hospital room was decorated with a large poster of Marilyn Monroe hung upside down, legs lubriciously akimbo. A Howdy Doody doll lay on the bed and the patient spent much time shooting at balloons with a popgun. Young women, discreetly described as "cousins", came and went at regular intervals. After his second operation Jackie arranged a prank in which film star Grace Kelly posed as a night nurse. But Jack was too ill to respond, leaving Kelly worried that her sex appeal might be slipping.

Jack finally left hospital with a suppurating wound in his back which healed only slowly. Dave Powers recalled that it was

as large as his fist. The crutches which were his constant companions caused big calluses under each armpit, and sometimes he had to be carried down steep flights of stairs.

The illness was a watershed in Jack's life. Early in 1954 he and Ted Sorensen had worked up an idea for an article about a number of American politicians who had taken courageous stands in the face of adversity. The long period in hospital gave Jack the chance to develop the article into a book, *Profiles in Courage*, a lucidly written collection of studies covering the political spectrum: John Quincy Adams, Daniel Webster, Thomas Hart Benton, Sam Houston, Edward G. Ross, Lucius Q.C. Lamar, George Norris and Robert Taft. The principal theme of the book was that politicians should not allow themselves to be the slaves of public opinion, and that on occasion caution under pressure was as courageous as outspoken idealism.

Profiles in Courage was published early in 1956 and rapidly became a best seller. In 1957 it won the Pulitzer Prize for Biography. The young senator from Massachusetts had not only fulfilled the promise he had shown in *Why England Slept* but had also reminded readers that, as a war hero, he knew a little about courage, too, and the Hemingway quality of "grace under pressure" to which he alluded in the book's first sentence.

Subsequently there were suggestions from some quarters that *Profiles in Courage* was not written solely by Jack, as the Kennedys have always maintained, but owed much to

Ted Sorensen's shaping hand, and to advice from a team of distinguished scholars including Jules David and James MacGregor Burns. When Jack first met his future Secretary of Defense, Robert McNamara, the latter startled him by inquiring if, indeed, he was the sole author of the book. Ted Sorensen, cited as Jack's "research assistant" in the book's preface, stoutly defended Kennedy's authorship, which relied heavily on dictation. Some historians, notably Herbert S. Parmet, have also argued persuasively that the hand of the ambassador can be detected in the award of the Pulitzer Prize. But the case for a "fix" – the prize's panel did not include *Profiles in Courage* in their recommendation but was overruled by the Pulitzer Advisory Board – is not proven.

At the time the publication and success of *Profiles in Courage* did Jack Kennedy no harm with the "high-class people". In 1956 he was asked to narrate *The Pursuit of Happiness*, a film produced by Dore Schary which was to open the Democratic Convention in Chicago. This was flattering, but Jack was aiming at a higher prize, the vice-presidential spot alongside the likely presidential candidate, the former governor of Illinois, Adlai Stevenson.

The Kennedy camp calculated that Jack's presence on the ticket would help Stevenson to win Catholic votes and would also deflect charges from the right that the Democrats were soft on Communism. At the same time, Jack buffed up his relatively modest liberal

Senator Kennedy signing copies of Profiles in
Courage. *In the spring of 1957 Jack followed
the book's success with the chairmanship of a
special Senate Committee to name the five
greatest senators in American history.* Profiles
in Courage *was awarded the Pulitzer Prize on
6 May 1957.*

credentials by taking a firm and well-publicized stand on the issue of civil rights, urging the Democratic Party to give unequivocal support to the Supreme Court's Brown decision of 1954 which ended segregation in schools. In Massachusetts he fought a no-holds-barred battle to defeat anti-Stevenson forces and install his own man, Pat Lynch, as state committee chairman.

In spite of heavy lobbying by the Kennedys, Stevenson remained unconvinced. He neither liked nor trusted the ambassador and considered that Jack's Catholicism, poor health and inexperience were potentially fatal drawbacks.

Jack arrived in Chicago at the head of the Massachusetts delegation and accompanied by the eight-months pregnant Jackie. He told reporters, "I am not a candidate, and I am not campaigning for office." Nevertheless, he indicated that he would accept the vice-presidential nomination should Stevenson select him.

When Jack delivered the speech nominating Stevenson, he moved closer to becoming Adlai's running mate. But the Kennedys' lock on the prize was loosened when, in a decision which Lyndon Johnson later called "the goddamned stupidest move a politician could make", Stevenson threw the vice-presidential nomination to the floor.

The next twelve hours were a maelstrom of frantic lobbying in which Jack came within an ace of seizing the nomination from his two principal rivals, Senators Hubert Humphrey and Estes Kefauver. This was the perfect opportunity for a demonstration of Kennedy competitiveness. At one point a Boston newsman traveling in a cab with Jack watched him clenching his fists and intoning "Go! Go! Go!" as they sped toward the convention hall. On the second ballot, as Lyndon Johnson announced that "Texas proudly casts its vote for the fighting sailor who wears the scars of battle", Jack raced ahead of Kefauver by 618 to 551 votes. He needed only 68 more for the nomination, but the Kennedy offensive had spent itself. Amid scenes of tumult and confusion on the convention floor the pendulum swung back to Kefauver and within minutes he went over the top.

Jack took the defeat without breaking stride. Ted Sorensen remembered: "Jack said, 'That's it – Let's go.' He wanted to get out of there fast and make the speech to give Kefauver unanimous support. He seemed to have no regrets. His idea was always to get on with the next thing."

In the long run, this rare example of a Kennedy failure was the making of Jack's political career. During the dramatic race for the nomination Jack's handsome face, clean-cut and smiling even in exhausted defeat, had imprinted itself on the minds of millions of television viewers. James MacGregor Burns considered that Jack had passed through "a kind of political sound barrier" and that "in this moment of defeat his campaign for the Presidency was born".

Failure spared Jack the landslide defeat which buried Stevenson and Kefauver and would almost certainly have consigned him to political oblivion if he had beaten Kefauver for the place on the ticket. It also released him from the lingering gravitational pull exerted by the memory of Joe Jr. Reflecting on his defeat at the convention, Jack concluded with a melancholy realism: "Joe was the star of our family. He did everything better than the rest of us. If he had lived, he would have gone on in politics, and he would have been elected to the House and to the Senate, as I was. And, like me, he would have gone for the vice-presidential nomination at the 1956 convention, but, unlike me, he wouldn't have been beaten. Joe would have won the nomination. And then he and Stevenson would have been beaten by Eisenhower, and today Joe's political career would be in shambles, and he would be trying to pick up the pieces."

The choice of the Massachusetts delegates but not that of the convention. Jack Kennedy at the 1956 Democratic convention, where he narrowly failed to secure the vice-presidential nomination. Success would in all probability have spelt the end of his political career.

Chapter Four

One Hell of a Candidate

JFK taking leave of Jackie at the airport, a familiar scene in the late 1950s when he was already running hard for the presidential nomination in 1960. Jack's relentless criss-crossing of the country laid the foundations of his drive for the presidency but also encouraged some criticism of his absenteeism record in the Senate.

Nothing explains the relationship between Jack Kennedy and his father more graphically than a snapshot from Jack's 1952 Senate race against Henry Cabot Lodge Jr. While Jack debated Lodge in a packed auditorium the ambassador, sitting high above in the gallery, frantically scribbled notes to be taken down to his son.

From the moment Jack was launched on his political career in 1946, the ambassador had been backing out of the limelight without entirely dispelling the suspicion that he was still pulling the strings from the wings. During the 1956 Democratic convention he had removed himself to a rented villa in the South of France, but the telephone wires burned hot at the height of the battle for the vice-presidency.

In 1957 Lem Billings gained a dramatic insight into the ambassador's strategic role in Jack's career. At a dinner party in the Kennedys' Palm Beach home Lem and Jack were trading jokes about the latter's sexual adventures when they were interrupted by a furious ambassador. Rounding on Billings, the ambassador told him: " You're not going to speak like that any more. There are things that you just can't bring up any more, private things. You've got to forget them. Forget the 'Jack' you once knew. From now on you've got to watch everything you say. The day is coming, and it's coming soon, when he won't be 'Jack' any more at all not to you and not to the rest of us either. He'll be 'Mr President'. And you can't say or do anything that will jeopardize that."

Above: Jack's physical grace is captured here as he relaxes in thoughtful mood in his four-room apartment at 122 Bowdoin Street which he rented to establish a Boston residence. Dave Powers recalled that the apartment had the atmosphere of a gentleman's club.
Opposite:JFK makes time for an interview at UCLA after a speech in 1957.

Jack's campaign for the presidency began immediately after his defeat at the 1956 Democratic convention and ended triumphantly four years later in the White House. Planned and purposeful to a degree which outmaneuvered and outwitted far more experienced political professionals than the young candidate, it was all the more remarkable for shaping a formidable contender from material which many at first considered markedly unpresidential. Reflecting on those days Lyndon Johnson

expressed the bafflement he felt at the way Jack caught the public imagination: "It was the goddamnest thing, here was this young whippersnapper, malaria-ridden and yellow, sickly, sickly ... Now I will admit that he had a good sense of humor and that he looked good on television ... but his growing hold on the American people was simply a mystery to me." In 1956 Jack still lacked political "bottom". He was not, and never would be, a member of the Senate's "inner circle". His youth and inexperience counted against him, as did his

Above: Hyannis sport. Jack releases a long pass to Jackie. On her left Eunice's clenched fists indicate Kennedy determination. Jackie was always uncomfortable with these strenuous Kennedy pastimes. "If I get the ball, which way do I run?" she asked after one huddle. After breaking an ankle playing touch football she withdrew to the sidelines. Opposite: Beach boys. Bobby, Jack and Teddy in one of a series of photographs taken for Look *magazine which brought the Kennedy family to a wide public in all their seductive glamor.*

Catholicism; when he had made his bid for the vice-presidential nomination, the ambassador had warned him that if he won the nomination and then went down with Stevenson, the defeat would in part be blamed on his Catholicism and frustrate his hopes for the bigger prize in 1960.

Nevertheless, his showing at the convention had turned Jack into a television personality. The camera liked him. Gracious in defeat and moving to make Kefauver the vice-presidential candidate by acclamation, Jack provided a nationwide television audience with a preview of the clipped tones and distinctive body language – the chopping hand and the stabbing forefinger – which

The Kennedys entertain at their Georgetown home. Bobby and his wife Ethel are on Jackie's right while Lem Billings makes an animated point at the far end of the table on Jack's right. Jackie filled the Georgetown house with 18th-century furniture and a large collection of paintings and drawings.

Jack cuddles Caroline, who was born on 27 November 1957. Their son John was born on 25 November 1960. A second son, Patrick, was born on 7 August 1963 but lived only two days.

would become increasingly familiar.

The award of the Pulitzer Prize in May 1957 also enhanced his profile, as did the Kennedys' artful cultivation of the press. A 1957 *Time* cover story which described Jack as the "Democratic whiz" of that year owed much to the ambassador's long friendship with Henry Luce. The endless stream of photo-essays which covered the Kennedys from 1957 to 1960 owed everything to their uniquely photogenic qualities as a family. Little arm-

twisting by Joe Kennedy was needed as Jack and Jackie extended unprecedented access to chosen writers and photographers, who repaid the favor by portraying them at work and play in all their seductive glamor. *Life* magazine pictured Jackie, cool and elegant, living her "cultured, quiet and apolitical life" at the the Kennedys' new Georgetown home while her husband was out on the stump. Baby daughter Caroline, born on 27 November 1957 and a bewitching little bundle, enabled the camera of

Life's Mark Shaw to catch Jack's unaffected display of fatherly pride. In the autumn of 1959 *Look* magazine produced a big feature on the Kennedy family which opened with a shot of Jack, Bobby and Teddy emerging from the surf, laughing, athletic and handsome, symbols of American self-confidence and proof of how far the Kennedys had traveled in three generations – proof of the American Dream itself.

To complete his political journey Jack had to underpin the photo-imagery with some political substance. He had always been his own man in the realm of foreign affairs, at early odds with his father, the doggedly isolationist Joe Kennedy, over his support for the Marshall Plan and the Truman Doctrine, which offered US aid to nations resisting either direct or indirect Communist aggression. He continued to speak out on Vietnam, in 1956 calling it "the cornerstone of the Free World in Southeast Asia", and from 1957 made good strategic use of the Seat on the Senate Foreign Relations Committee which Majority Leader Lyndon Johnson had given him after relentless badgering by the ambassador. As a member of the Committee, Jack turned his attention to another of France's colonies, Algeria, where since 1954 a French army of 450,000 men had been fighting a full-scale guerrilla war against the nationalist Front de Liberation National (FLN). In a well-publicized Senate speech he urged President Eisenhower to recognize that in spite of French insistence that the war in Algeria was an "internal matter", the Algerian war of independence represented a threat to the stability of the Western world. Kennedy urged that the United States should use its influence to secure a settlement which would "shape a course of political independence" for the Algerians.

The French were considerably put out by Kennedy's intervention, calling on the State Department to repudiate his views. Visiting Paris, Adlai Stevenson made a speech in which he suggested that Kennedy's speech had imperiled the unity of NATO. Dubbed "the Senator for Algeria", Jack remained unruffled by all this huffing and puffing. In an article in Foreign Affairs he accused the Eisenhower administration of failing to grasp how fast the forces of nationalism were "rewriting the geopolitical map of the world".

As a congressman Jack had always been a supporter of a vigorous defense policy. In 1948–9 he had attacked the Truman administration over the economies it had made in the defense establishment, advocating an air force of 70 groups rather than the 55 groups proposed by Secretary of Defense Louis Johnson. As a Cold War warrior in the 1950s, he had urged the re-arming of Europe, if necessary with US help, and the concentration of "as large a proportion as possible of our national production to our air program". In the Senate in the summer of 1954 he had opposed the Eisenhower administration's reduction in the size of the army as inimical to "our national security and our responsible leadership in world affairs". In May 1955,

After 1956 JFK became the most sought-after political speaker in the United States. In the first six months of 1958 he received 2,568 invitations to speak and accepted 96. He wryly observed, "If I decide to run in '60, I will at least have been around and met a lot of people in different parts of the country."

returning to the Senate after his long illness, he claimed that the administration had "guessed short" on the military strength of the Soviet Union, and that further reductions in the US armed forces were ill-conceived.

It was by this consistent route that in 1958 Jack Kennedy arrived at the momentous discovery of the "missile gap", which was to provide one of the principal themes of his 1960 presidential campaign. In the early 1950s the United States and the Soviet Union had begun to concentrate on missile development, aimed at producing a weapon capable of carrying a nuclear warhead. By 1957 American scientists had successfully tested the Jupiter intermediate range ballistic missile, with a range of over 3,000 miles, but had still not carried out trials with long-range strategic missiles. The Russians, however, had successfully tested two long-range missiles, and on 4 October 1957 launched the satellite Sputnik I into space.

The tinny little bleeps from Sputnik produced a powerful feeling of unease in the United States. There was a widespead fear that the apparent Soviet lead in rocketry – the so-called "missile gap" – had exposed a loss of American technological superiority which had been taken for granted since 1945. No one questioned the basis on which the "gap" had been calculated, and when Jack Kennedy became president it became clear that it did not exist. Kennedy's reaction was to continue as if it did.

In 1957 Sputnik represented not only a Soviet threat but also a big stick with which to beat the Republican Party without launching a counterproductive attack on the benign, almost papal figure of Eisenhower. It has been suggested that initially Jack Kennedy failed to understand the symbolic power of the issue, merely seizing on it as a means of extracting increased defense spending in New England industries hit by unemployment. But it did not take long for him to couch his argument in a style which recalls the analysis in *Why England Slept* of the democracies' failure to re-arm in the 1930s. On 14 August 1958, in a major speech in the Senate, he warned that if the United States made the same mistake, "... the deterrent ratio might well shift to the Soviets so heavily, during the years of the gap, as to open to them a shortcut to world domination ... Their missile power will be the shield from behind which they will slowly, but surely advance – through Sputnik diplomacy, limited 'brush fire' wars, indirect non-overt aggression, intimidation and subversion, internal revolution, increased prestige or influence, and the vicious blackmail of our allies. The periphery of the free world will shift against us."

Invoking Winston Churchill, he concluded by exhorting the Senate, "Come then – let us to the task, to the battle and to the toil – each to our own part, each to our station." In this self-conscious rhetoric lie the seeds of Kennedy's inaugural address: the warning of great danger, the summons to sacrifice, and the appeal over the heads of his political peers to the nation to unite in a common purpose on a heroic adventure – the essence of the "voluntary totalitarianism" of which he had written eighteen years before in *Why England Slept*.

Jack had always set a higher priority on foreign affairs rather than on domestic issues, but his political ambitions obliged him to place his views on domestic problems in sharper focus. His conduct over the the censure of McCarthy had not endeared him to the liberals. By sidestepping the issue at every turn he had avoided being fouled by the McCarthy tar-baby, which had besmirched both the senator's enemies and defenders. But Jack's apparent indifference to the human cost of McCarthy's rampage, and particularly the deep and lasting wounds he had inflicted on the State Department, were hardly consistent with the flinty individualism celebrated by the author of *Profiles in Courage* – more profile than courage as some critics later observed.

The problems posed by civil rights, which since 1945 had risen steadily toward the top of the political agenda, presented another potential minefield for an ambitious politician. The ambivalence of the White House, the deep hostility to reform shown by the conservative coalition of Southern Democrats and Midwestern Republicans in Congress, and the lip service paid to the concept of racial equality by the majority of white Americans, recommended a cautious approach. Jack Kennedy maneuvered to please liberals and to soothe voters in the South, where his

JFK with his secretary Evelyn Lincoln, who began working for him in 1952 and became his personal secretary in 1953, a position she held until his death.

Catholicism was likely to be seen as an electoral liability. The liberals were heartened by his support for the most controversial provision of the 1957 Civil Rights Bill, which gave the Justice Department greater powers and failed to pass, and were then dismayed when Kennedy voted for a Southern amendment which required cases of criminal contempt to be tried by juries, ensuring that local segregationists would have the last word. This smacked of expediency. Privately, Jack reassured important Southern politicians that he had a "pragmatic" approach to the problems of civil rights.

The principal domestic issue over which Jack Kennedy extended himself during his senatorial career was that of labor reform. In 1957–8 he served on the McClellan Committee, which was probing the involvement of the Teamsters Union in labor racketeering. It was not entirely coincidental that chief counsel to the Committee was Robert Kennedy, in hot pursuit of the Teamsters' boss Jimmy Hoffa. This, too, might have proved a bed of nails, for although the Teamsters were linked with the Grand Old Party, the Democratic Party had close overall ties with organized labor. However, Jack's seat on the committee conferred several important advantages. He benefited from his association with his brother's relentless crusade against Hoffa, forged links with the United Auto Workers Union, sheltering from the storm in the lee of the Democratic Party, and opened up lines to the national press which were his own rather

than his father's. A final bonus came with Jack's chairmanship of the Labor Subcommittee, which led to his introduction in June 1958 of a bill setting out comprehensive reforms to deal with corruption and malpractice by both management and unions. After a stormy reception the bill was supported overwhelmingly by union leaders – with the significant exception of Jimmy Hoffa. It passed the Senate by 88 votes to one but was then bogged down in a procedural quagmire by the unsympathetic Eisenhower administration. For Jack Kennedy, however, his work on the Committee and the bill had given him a leading position on one of the most pressing domestic issues of the day and demonstrated his goodwill toward the unions while suggesting that he was no mere Prince Charming but a politician of substance.

In 1958 Jack's re-election as senator for a second term by nearly one million votes, the greatest majority in Massachusetts history, provided the launching pad for his still unannounced presidential bid, but in true Kennedy fashion the organization was already in place. While coyly denying any presidential ambitions, Jack was running hard in a nationwide version of the sweeps which in the early 1950s had helped to secure Massachusetts.

Journalist Carleton V. Kent recalled, "... all of a sudden he began popping up all around the country making speeches in farm communities and other areas – conservation areas – where a Massachusetts' senator would

Jack and Bobby look pensive during the hearings of the McClellan Committee as Teamsters president Dave Beck takes the Fifth Amendment. Bobby later said of his brother's decision to serve on the Committee: " ... the Kennedys were involved in investigating labor unions at a time when labor and the Democratic party were very close to one another. He thought it was the correct thing to do, and so he went ahead."

not be supposed to have any great interest. It was perfectly plain what he was doing, and he did it very well."

By mid-1959 his headquarters was well established in a suite in the Esso Building in Washington. Here another "honorary Kennedy", brother-in-law Stephen Smith, who had married Jean Kennedy in 1956, presided over serried ranks of filing cabinets bulging with state-by-state lists of thousands of potential supporters from governors to local

committee men and grass-roots voters. According to James MacGregor Burns: "Coded card files and invitation lists were used to prepare thousands of letters expressing Kennedy's pleasure at having met people on his trips. New gray filing cabinets were packed with polls and electoral studies, press releases, newspaper clippings and other political intelligence. In a corner office overlooking the Capitol, Smith and an assistant were in almost continuous telephone calls with politicians across the country... As they talked, they could study wall maps broken down into congressional, county and local political jurisdictions ..." It was the method first applied to the Eleventh Congressional District of Massachusetts blown up to a national scale.

Jack now revealed a growing mastery of political detail. As early as 1957 he was able to jab his finger at any area on a map of the United States and then reel off from memory a list of the most influential people living there. To augment the loyal team which had served him from the early days, Kennedy began hiring campaign staff as soon as the Massachusetts election was over. Attention was paid to recruiting the right people at every level. In *The Kennedy Promise* Henry Fairlie described a chance meeting on the underground railroad of the Senate office between Jack Kennedy and Jerry Bruno. Jack remembered Bruno from a meeting in Wisconsin two years earlier, asked him to his Georgetown home the following morning and there suggested to Bruno that "I go to work full time for him, organizing in Wisconsin in case he decided to run in that state's primary. There was no doubt he was running for President."

The perfected version of the "campaign before the campaign" was made possible by the wealth of the ambassador, who in July 1959 purchased and leased to Jack through a subsidiary of Kennedy Enterprises a luxurious Convair jet which was quickly christened *Caroline*. That autumn *Caroline* carried Jack to appearances in twenty-two states. By October

he and Ted Sorensen had met more than half the potential delegates to the 1960 convention.

Later some commentators ascribed to the Kennedy machine a new "scientific" approach to campaigning. In truth the Kennedys were not so much innovators as super-efficient exploiters of every political weapon to hand: from the ambassador's behind-the-scenes wheeling and dealing with shady but powerful figures best screened from Jack, to the employment of men like Lou Harris, master of the new pseudoscience of opinion polling. It was pointless for the Kennedys' opponents to castigate them for the expenditure of vast sums. Money was at the very root of the American political system, and to run everyone had perforce to dig into their pockets and those of their supporters – the Kennedy pockets were just deeper. The inestimable advantage which Jack drew from his father's munificence was that he never had to worry about finding the cash to meet an unexpected eventuality. It was all there before he started.

Jack declared his candidacy for the presidency in the Senate Caucus Room on 2 January 1960. He ruled out the possibility of accepting the vice-presidential nomination, and said that he intended to enter several primaries. He concluded by striking a note that would ring through the campaign and his presidency, declaring that it was his aim "to give direction to our troubled moral purpose, awakening every American to the dangers and opportunities that confront us". Jack's first real test came in Wisconsin's open primary, where his opponent

was Hubert Humphrey, the loquacious, populist liberal from neighbouring Minnesota. Having rejoined the Kennedy team as Jack's campaign manager, Bobby fought for victory as relentlessly as he had harried Jimmy Hoffa, plowing through the March snows of the Midwest and losing a pound a week in the process. Jack meanwhile steeled himself for what remained an ordeal, his "dawn to exhaustion schedule", pressing the flesh until his right hand was swollen and bleeding. The two brothers were a study in opposites: Jack sifting information and analyzing options with a computer-like calm; Bobby driven, testy and sparing no one, not even Jackie, who was a political innocent and dreaded campaigning. Watching Jack and his beautiful wife working opposite sides of a humdrum Wisconsin street, the journalist Joe Alsop likened them to "a little pair of lost children".

But it was Hubert Humphrey who lost his way. Regarded as "the third senator from Wisconsin", he nevertheless found himself battling uphill against the juggernaut efficiency of the Kennedy campaign. Bitterness lay behind his later mealy-mouthed summary of the contribution to the contest made by Jackie and Rose Kennedy: "They were queen and queen mother among the commoners, extracting obeisance, awe and respect. They lacked only tiaras, and you knew that if crowns were needed, Joe Kennedy would buy them. I felt like an independent merchant competing against a chain store."

Religion determined the indecisive

JFK in conversation with a journalist aboard Caroline *during the 1960 presidential campaign. Kennedy aides referred to these sessions as "confessionals".*

outcome of the Wisconsin primary. Jack won, taking 40 per cent of the popular vote and 56 per cent of the Democratic vote, but the split had followed Catholic-Protestant and urban-rural lines, with Jack's support coming from the cities and towns and the state's large population of German and Polish Catholics.

The issue of religion loomed large as the two rivals pressed on into impoverished, fundamentalist West Virginia for a climactic showdown. Catholics made up under 4 per cent of the population and pre-primary polls giving Jack a substantial lead were reversed when it became known that he was Catholic. Nevertheless, as Pierre Salinger, Kennedy's press secretary, was to observe later, had Humphrey dropped out after Wisconsin the Kennedy campaign might have foundered, as it needed just this kind of challenge to dramatize its themes and lay the religion bogey to rest:

"Kennedy might never have been able to demonstrate that he could overcome the Catholic issue. Had he faced no opposition, any victory there would have been meaningless in terms of bargaining with big-city bosses."

Hubert Humphrey helped by playing the religion card for all it was worth, even adopting *Give Me That Old Time Religion* as his campaign song. Jack responded by linking the religious argument to his wartime record, declaring, "Nobody asked me if I was a Catholic when I joined the United States Navy." For extra measure, he dragged in the shade of Joe Jr with a solemn reminder, "and nobody asked my brother whether he was a Catholic or a Protestant before he climbed into an American bomber to fly his last mission". There was some irony in this for, as Jackie pointed out, of all the Kennedys Jack was the one whose faith was purely nominal.

To charges that the Catholic church would be the unseen power behind his presidency, Jack gave a dramatic straight-to-camera reassurance during a telecast on the eve of the vote. "... When any man stands on the steps of the Capitol and takes the oath of office of President, he is swearing to support the separation of church and state; he puts one hand on the Bible and raises the other hand to God as he takes the oath. And if he breaks this oath, he is not only committing a crime against the Constitution, for which the Congress can impeach him – and should impeach him – but he is committing a sin against God." Then, raising his hand as if from an imaginary Bible,

Jack repeated in soft, measured tones, " a sin against God, for he has sworn on the Bible".

Hailed as a masterpiece of moving sincerity, Jack's words had been carefully planned and were given in response to a planted question. The West Virginia primary was a rich combination of high-flown sentiment and good old-fashioned mud-slinging. The Kennedy camp put out a press release hinting that Humphrey had been a draft dodger in the Second World War. In fact he had been rejected for military service on medical grounds. The charge was publicly withdrawn by Jack but the mud stuck, leaving voters to contemplate the contrived contrast between the heroic commander of *PT-109*, who was surrounded on the stump by his former crew members, and a devious politician unwilling to serve his country. The point was rammed home in a Kennedy-produced documentary which was shown statewide and which opened with a night-time shot of a speeding PT-boat leaving a phosphorescent glow in its wake.

Struggling to keep up with the Kennedys was the hapless Humphrey, bewailing the relative poverty of his campaign, railing against Jack as "papa's pet" and Bobby as a "young emotional juvenile". In part his frustration stemmed from the simple fact that he had less money with which to oil the notoriously corrupt electoral wheels of West Virginia. In 1966 Cardinal Cushing told Humphrey that he and the ambassador had "bought" the primary with heavy donations to selected Protestant ministers, unctuously

observing that "It's good for the Lord. It's good for the church. It's good for the preacher, and it's good for the candidate."

Mafia money, too, seems to have found its way into the Kennedy campaign chest, chaneled by a Chicago mobster named Sam Giancana, then living under the alias "Sam Flood", who was an acquaintance of Jack's friend Frank Sinatra. Doubtless Giancana's aim was to purchase protection from future federal probes into his activities and those of his associates.

At the legitimate level, the ambassador devised the masterstroke of the campaign. Franklin D. Roosevelt Jr, then working as a Washington car salesman, was drafted into West Virginia to invoke the memory of his father and the New Deal which had meant so much to the state in the 1930s. Clearly shocked by the deprivation he discovered in West Virginia, and eloquently responsive to it, Jack in turn became a youthful reincarnation of FDR. In a stroke of vulgar genius typical of Joe Kennedy, Roosevelt's endorsement letters were postmarked at Hyde Park, creating the fleeting impression that from beyond the grave FDR was supporting Jack's campaign. It was also Franklin D. Roosevelt Jr who put his name to the press statement branding Humphrey a draft dodger and who fed Jack the question about the separation of church and state.

When it came to the vote, religion was not the decisive factor. The West Virginians declined to confirm the popular belief that they were bigots and, having weighed up both

Bobby Kennedy and miners during the West
Virginia primary. JFK's opponent, Hubert
Humphrey, accused Bobby of being
"emotional" and "juvenile", a wild
underestimate of a relentless campaigner
dedicated to one thing and one thing only; the
election of his brother as President.

candidates, they decided that Jack Kennedy was the man more likely to defeat the Republicans and do something about the state's shattered economy. As Herbert Parmet has pointed out, they had been living with Catholic politicians at all levels for many years, and so they were quite happy to live with Jack Kennedy. Jack's 61 per cent of the popular vote and sweep of 48 of West Virginia's 55 counties knocked Humphrey out of the race and demonstrated that Jack's Catholicism would not be electorally fatal.

His victory in West Virginia carried Jack to the Democratic convention in Los Angeles as a seemingly invincible front runner. Having guarded his right flank with his tough anti-Communism and "pragmatic" approach to civil rights, Jack now began attracting liberal intellectuals whose previous loyalty had been to Adlai Stevenson. Many of them liked to think that they were pretty tough and pragmatic too, and Jack appeared to be "a Stevenson with balls". Ted Sorensen had been headhunting intellectuals since the winter of 1958 which saw the formation of an echo of Roosevelt's "brain trust", the Academic Advisory Committee, whose members included John Kenneth Galbraith, Arthur Schlesinger Jr and Walt Rostow. They were useful window dressing for the Kennedy campaign, but Jack had little time for what he called "professional liberals" and never considered himself one of them. His aim, successfully accomplished, was to occupy the center ground of American politics and then move out to embrace the wide range of liberal opinion to his left. His rhetoric encouraged the liberals to believe that he was on their side, while conservatives were comforted by his actions, which rarely ran counter to their important interests. Tip O'Neill wondered if Jack was a Democrat at all: "… looking back on his congressional campaign, and on his later campaigns for the Senate and then for the presidency, I'd have to say that he was only nominally a Democrat. He was a Kennedy, which was more than a family affiliation. It quickly developed into an entire political party, with its own people, its own approach, and its own strategies."

It was Jack's gift to appear to be a liberal while remaining a conservative; to be Catholic and without seeming to be so; and to be immensely rich without in any way appearing to be spoiled by it. His vigor betrayed none of the softness which often comes with such privilege, and his combination of coolness and approachability betrayed none of the rough edges and festering resentments which had driven his father. As journalist Murray Kempton observed, he was really "one hell of a candidate".

At the Democratic convention in July 1960, two obstacles blocked his nomination on the first ballot: Adlai Stevenson, hovering in the wings and threatening to play a wild card; and a more formidable opponent, Lyndon Johnson. Johnson believed that he could win without the primaries; if Stevenson could take Kennedy to a second ballot, then the Texan might make his move.

JFK on the stump in West Virginia during April 1960, using machinery of New Deal vintage as an impromptu platform. Many of the audience seem too young to vote, but they would go home and tell their mothers about Jack Kennedy. Jack romped home with 219,246 votes against Humphrey's 141,941.

Johnson was a complex character, thin-skinned and rancorous, fawning one moment, foul-mouthed the next. He had no love for the Kennedys, denouncing the ambassador as "the man who had held Chamberlain's umbrella at Munich", calling Jack "a little scrawny fellow with rickets", and fomenting the revelations about his Addison's disease. Ironically, there were doubts about Johnson's own health, as he was not yet recovered from a massive heart attack.

When Jack accepted a challenge to debate Johnson before the Texas delegation, the Senate Majority Leader assumed a more accommodating public face, introducing his rival as "a man of unusually high character". Johnson harried Jack to the bitter end. Stevenson had the sentimental sympathy of the convention but few of the votes. Neither could prevent Jack winning on the first ballot with 808 votes to Johnson's 409. The Kennedy machine had killed the contest even before it began, and in the process had extracted much of the usual excitement from the convention. The politics of arithmetic had produced a feeling of anticlimax. Referring to the "synthetic hullaballoo" of the convention, Russell Baker of the New York Times noted, "the political connoisseurs here are talking in awe of the Kennedy machine's efficiency in coolly eliminating every element of the contest before the convention opened". And there was indeed a sharp contrast between the carefully fashioned image of Jack's sincerity and appeal to youthful idealism, and the ruthlessness of the campaign which secured him the presidential nomination.

With victory gained, Jack then precipitated an extraordinary muddle over his choice of running mate. Having offered the vice-presidency to Lyndon Johnson, he was besieged by an outraged Bobby and many of his campaign team to change his mind. In a sequence of emotional meetings bordering on farce Bobby attempted, apparently on his own initiative, to withdraw the offer, Lyndon Johnson burst into tears, Lady Bird Johnson had hysterics and Jack flapped around indecisively. The situation was retrieved after some brisk lectures on the telephone delivered by the ambassador and Johnson was retained on the ticket. While all the participants continued to sulk, the ambassador gave the glowering Jack and Bobby a valuable demonstration of insouciance and political insight, telling them, "Don't worry ... In two weeks everyone will be saying that this was the smartest thing you ever did." He was right. Without Johnson's ability to claim back Texas and Louisiana for the Democratic Party and to keep the Carolinas, Jack Kennedy would not have become president.

The force of Jack's acceptance speech was blunted by his evident exhaustion, but in it he coined a phrase which combined the symbol of America's continental expansion in the past with the global challenges of the new decade. "The New Frontier" would soon pass into the vernacular: "... we stand today on the edge of a New Frontier, the frontier of the 1960s, a

The Democratic Convention, July 1960, Los Angeles. Jack huddles with Bobby, his brother and campaign manager, and two strong supporters, Governor Abraham Ribicoff of Connecticut and Democratic Chairman John Bailey, who was later to become National Chairman. The strategic huddle concerned a decision of who would lead the delegation and whether to release the delegation to vote with their conscience after the first ballot.

frontier of unknown opportunities and paths, a frontier of unfulfilled hopes and threats... the New Frontier of which I speak is not a set of promises; it is a set of challenges. It sums up not what I intend to offer the American people, but what I intend to ask of them ... I am asking each of you to be pioneers on the New Frontier."

At the start of the presidential campaign Jack's striking vision of the New Frontier became an albatross around his neck, as he struggled to define exactly what it was and where it lay. Temporarily he had tripped himself up with his growing oratorical mastery. In the polls he was trailing his Republican opponent, Richard M. Nixon, Eisenhower's vice-president, principally because of the exposure Nixon had received at the Republican convention a month after Jack's victory at Los Angeles. Nor did there seem to be much to choose between the two candidates. The television journalist Eric Sevareid characterized both men as products of the managerial revolution, politicians in gray flannel suits who were "tidy buttoned-down men... completely packaged products".

The Soviet leader Nikita Khrushchev put the dilemma more earthily, dismissing Kennedy and Nixon as "a pair of boots – which is the better, the right boot or the left boot?" To put some daylight between the candidates, Arthur Schlesinger produced a booklet entitled "Kennedy or Nixon: Does It Make Any Difference?" – a question which never could have been asked of Stevenson and Eisenhower

– in which he dismissed Nixon as a mendacious, sentimental vulgarian and described Kennedy as an "exceptionally cerebral figure" and "a committed liberal".

On 26 September 1960 a single event broke the logjam – the first of four televised debates between the presidential contenders. Neither man was a stranger to the medium. Nixon was the veteran of the lachrymose "Checkers" speech which in 1952 had saved his political career, and the victor by a technical knock-out in the famous "kitchen debate" with the abrasive Khrushchev. Kennedy had made effective use of televison in the campaign against Henry Cabot Lodge Jr, and from 1956 had become something of a television star.

Jack had been carefully prepared and made up for the first encounter with Nixon, which was watched by an audience of 60 million. If, as Marshall McLuhan believed, television was a "hot" medium, then Jack Kennedy was one of the coolest practitioners of low-pressure presentation. Handsome, composed and in control, he displayed no sign of effort. Sweating under the studio lights, and in some pain from a knee injury, the wretched Nixon appeared jowly and ill at ease, trying too hard. Watching the debate, McLuhan thought that Nixon resembled, "the railway lawyer who signs leases that are not in the best interests of the folks in the little town". Norman Mailer remembered him as "a church usher, of the variety who would twist a boy's ear after removing him from the church".

Neither man said anything very

Right: The morning after JFK won his party's nomination for the Presidency a stream of powerful Democrats came to push their man for vice president. There were fourteen in the running ranging in ideology from Adlai Stevenson, Chester Bowles and "Soapy" Williams of Michigan on the left to Henry "Scoop" Jackson on the right. Given the close race against Nixon expected, and knowing the importance of the Electoral Votes of Texas, Kennedy decided to offer the vice presidency to Lyndon Johnson, who was not a candidate. Against the wishes of Bobby Kennedy and to the surprise of many Johnson supporters, Lyndon accepted. This picture was taken at that private meeting, long before it was announced to the delegates and the press. Overleaf: JFK speaking in Detroit at the start of the presidential campaign. The great rhetorical flourishes which embellished his inaugural address, particularly his evocation of the "New Frontier", made a tentative appearance in his early campaign speeches, but were only to crystallize as the campaign wore on and Kennedy's confidence grew.

memorable – this was an age before the "sound bite" – and a majority of people listening to the debate on the radio considered that Nixon had shaded it. The television audience was seduced by the relaxed image of Kennedy, and through the strange alchemy of the medium felt that somehow they had got to know him personally. Viewers were repelled by the contrasting sharpness of Nixon's image, which conveyed his edginess, hunger and self-doubts. The baleful eye of the camera had uncovered the "real" Nixon but had slid around the smooth surface of the urbane Kennedy. It was a disaster for Nixon. McLuhan believed that without television "Nixon had it made".

After the first television debate Jack hit his stride. The hurried monotone into which he often slipped during a speech was replaced by a more confident timbre. David Halberstam observed: "That harsh New England tone, which at first had jarred others, seemed to soften a little at the very same time that the nation began to find it distinctive and began to listen for it."

Kennedy motorcades were generating intense excitement, particularly from the women who lined the route. As early as 1956, when Jack had campaigned for Adlai Stevenson, young women had screamed at him, "You're better than Elvis!" Now his passage sparked what the press corps labeled the "jumpers", women of all ages leaping with unrestrained excitement as Jack drove by. Then there were the "clutchers", women who crossed their arms and hugged themselves

shouting "He looked at me!"; and the "runners", often with a child in tow, who pursued the car down the street.

The Kennedy team choreographed this near-hysteria for the cameras. Jerry Bruno recounted: "It happened in Detroit ... As soon as the plane landed and Kennedy stepped out of the doorway, the crowd began to push forward. They knocked down the snow fence and swarmed all over Kennedy... 'My God,' Kennedy said afterward, 'I can't believe that crowd. How did you do it?' I couldn't believe it either. But it looked so good on film and in the press that from then on we made sure that the crowds surged over Kennedy. I'd have two men holding a rope by an airport or along a motorcade; then, at the right time, they'd just drop the rope and the crowd would rush close to Kennedy... it was one of those things that just happened." The positive images of Jack's youth and vigor, rather than any specific policies, were now contrasted with an enervated Eisenhower administration. Its exhaustion and bankruptcy of ideas was symbolized by the web of denials and admissions, disavowals and blustering which had followed the shooting down of an American U-2 reconnaissance aircraft over the Soviet Union in May 1961, an embarrassment which turned to ashes Eisenhower's hopes of a summit with Khrushchev. Jack's campaign slogan, "Let's Get This Country Moving Again", coined by Walt Rostow, promised an antidote to the blandness and quietism of the Eisenhower years and coincidentally caught

Right: Medium and message. The candidates during the last of their four TV debates. By now Nixon was handling himself more confidently in front of the cameras, but he never recovered from the disaster of the first debate. Above: JFK's popularity continued to grow.

Above: The Kennedy magic at work in Los Angeles as JFK's motorcade pushes through a sea of clutching hands. In the front seat, basking in the reflected glory, is the Governor of California, Pat Brown. Right: By 1960 Jack Kennedy had been transformed from the hesitant tyro politician of 1946 into one of the most gifted and attractive campaigners American politics has ever seen. The blizzards of confetti which regularly rained down on his motorcades were sometimes so heavy that when the doors of his convertible were opened the paper poured out like water from a tank. Opposite: Jack Kennedy's abundant natural charm is caught as he turns to greet a traffic cop while campaigning in New York's Harlem district.

the groundswell of social change that had been stirring since the mid-1950s. Richard Nixon remained hopelessly square, but Jack Kennedy, while no member of the rock'n' roll generation, could have stepped straight off the album cover of Frank Sinatra's *Songs for Swinging Lovers*.

Still Nixon clung on, a sitting target for Jack's elegant, sniping wit and the recipient of some eccentric support from Eisenhower. Asked by newsmen to nominate the important decisions in which Nixon had played a part, Ike replied,"Give me a week and I might come up with something." At the end of October a Gallup poll gave Kennedy a small lead of 49 per cent to 46. The Catholic issue still dogged Jack, demanding a repeat of the reassurances he had given the electorate during the West Virginia primary. On 12 September, in a speech at Houston, he had declared, "Contrary to common newspaper usage, I am not the Catholic candidate for President. I am the Democratic Party's candidate for President."

Crucial to the outcome was the contest for the black vote. Nixon, who began the campaign with better credentials than

Opposite: The Kennedys Are Coming, releasing a pent-up wave of excitement clearly visible on the faces of the female members of the crowd. Right: A young Kennedy supporter with a blunt message for Mamie Eisenhower. During the final days of the presidential campaign, as Richard Nixon narrowed the gap between himself and JFK, the support the latter enjoyed among voters under thirty proved crucial to the outcome.

Kennedy on this issue, handled it badly. Matters came to a head in Atlanta on 19 October. During a sit-in campaign against the city's entrenched segregationist practices the leader of the Southern Christian Leadership Conference, Dr Martin Luther King, was arrested. Already on parole after being arrested on the trumped-up charge of driving without a Georgia license, King was sentenced to four months in Reidsville State Penitentiary.

Nixon privately asked the Justice Department to determine whether King's constitutional rights had been violated, but declined to make a public statement on behalf of the SCLC leader. For his own part Jack Kennedy had handled this political hot potato by cutting a deal with the Democratic governor of Georgia, Ernest Vandiver, that in return for King's speedy release he would make no public statement. However, on the urging of Kennedy aide Harris Wofford, who maintained close links with the civil rights movement, and Sargent Shriver, the campaign team's civil rights coordinator, Jack agreed to make a telephone call to King's wife Coretta to express his sympathy. In a short exchange he told her, "I'm thinking of you and your husband, and I know this must be a very difficult time for you."

Bobby exploded when he heard of the call, claiming that if news of it leaked out it would cost Jack at least three southern states. The next day, in calmer mood, he took the ethically questionable decision to ring the judge who

had sentenced King to secure his release. Twenty-four hours later King was a free man.

Outside the prison, King, somewhat over-generously, gave Jack the entire credit for his release, praising him as a man of principle and providing him with everything short of an official endorsement. King's father, a Republican, declared, "It's time for all of us to take off our Nixon buttons." The Kennedy campaign rushed out two million pamphlets with details of the affair and a headline which read "No Comment Nixon vs. A Candidate with Heart". They were distributed in black schools and, on the Sunday before the election, outside black churches. According to a post-election Gallup poll, Kennedy received 68 per cent of the black vote.

Accompanied by the heavily pregnant Jackie, Jack cast his vote in Boston on the morning of 8 November. Afterward the couple flew to the family compound at Hyannis Port. Waiting for the first returns to come in, the family played touch football on the lawn.

Tension ran high in the Hyannis Port communications room, which was crammed with lines of telephones, ranks of teletypes and banks of television screens. Throughout the night the predictions spewed out by the CBS election computer seesawed back and forth. By 11pm it looked as if Jack would win by a popular vote of over a million. Then Nixon clawed his way back in Oklahoma, Virginia and Ohio and ran neck and neck in Wisconsin and Michigan. It was clear that victory would be achieved only by the narrowest of margins.

Anxiety is plainly visible on Jack's face, and on Jackie's, as his motorcade noses through New York's garment district toward the end of the campaign. An enthusiastic member of the crowd has grabbed his arm and won't let go, a real threat to his weak back. The crush of the crowd was so great that the doors of Kennedy's car buckled. This was the heavily pregnant Jackie's last campaign appearance with her husband.

In the small hours of 9 November Jack surged ahead again, but was then pegged back in the Midwest. He was now a tantalizing two electoral votes away from the presidency, but in the South the Democrats had voted for independent candidates, leaving 26 electoral votes pledged to no one. It seemed as if the contest would be decided in the House of Representatives, as neither Kennedy or Nixon would have a majority. If that happened, it would be "one state, one vote", and the spoils would go to the candidate the South considered the most "pragmatic" on segregation.

At 6am, while Kennedy and Nixon slept and Bobby Kennedy remained hunched over the telephone in the Hyannis Port communications room, Associated Press bulletins confirmed that Jack had won in Michigan, giving him 285 electoral votes, enough to claim victory. At midday Nixon conceded defeat, sending his aide Herb Klein to read a statement. Jack dismissed his opponent with the cutting jibe, "He went out the way he came in – no class."

When the final figures were revealed Jack had won 49.7 of the popular vote and Nixon had taken 49.6. Of the 68, 838, 979 votes cast, only 112, 803 separated the candidates; no presidential election has ever been as close. Much was subsequently made of the evident electoral fraud in Cook County, Illinois, sanctioned by Chicago's Mayor Richard Daley, an old friend of the ambassador, and abetted by mobsters like Sam Giancana, but it

had no effect on the electoral vote. More important to securing Jack's victory was the presence on the Democratic ticket of Lyndon Johnson, his own last-minute appeal to the black vote and his appeal to voters under the age of thirty. In spite of the impressive reassurances he had given in the Democratic primaries and the race against Nixon, Jack had failed to bury the issue of religion. Indeed, at the beginning of the presidential campaign he had great difficulty in securing the endorsement of a number of important Catholic leaders, who feared that Jack's candidacy might provoke an anti-Catholic backlash. At the end of the day, however, the Catholic vote held up.

On the morning of 9 November the time-honored ritual of touch football was resumed on the Hyannis Port lawn. Jack joined Jackie for a walk on the wind-blown dunes and then posed for photographers, lifting Caroline on to his shoulders, a feat he only achieved with some difficulty. Screened by secret service men, the family traveled to the Hyannis Port Armory, where Jack made a nationally televised victory statement. Appearing for the first time in public with his son for many years was the ambassador, mission accomplished. Jack told newsmen that the nation could now prepare for a new administration, while he prepared for a new baby.

J F K and Jackie on 8 November 1960 after casting their votes in Boston.

Mr President

"Let the word go forth from this time and place ... that the torch has been passed to a new generation of Americans." John F. Kennedy delivering his inaugural speech.

The inauguration of an American president is a solemn and austere affair. The raw winter weather in which it is held chills the body and concentrates the mind. Arthur Schlesinger began his memoir of Jack Kennedy by setting the scene for the ceremony: "It all began in the cold. It had been cold all week in Washington. Then early Thursday afternoon came the snow. The wind blew in icy, stinging gusts and whipped the snow down the frigid streets."

On 19 January, the day before the inauguration, eight inches of snow fell, blanketing the green dye which had been sprayed on the lawns around the Washington Monument to invest the ceremony with a suggestion of imminent spring. As the temperature plummeted, 3,000 servicemen worked through the night with plows to sweep the thoroughfares clear of snow. In dawn's light, army flame throwers were used to melt the remaining ice on the streets and sidewalks. The inauguration, watched by an audience of 20,000 people gathered outside the east front of the Capitol, began at midday, 20 January 1961. It lasted a little over fifty minutes, twenty-eight of which were taken up by the prayers of four clergymen, the most long-winded being the old Kennedy ally, Richard Cardinal Cushing, whose benedictions were accompanied by wisps of smoke sent up by some faulty wiring in the lectern. The aged cardinal was followed by the 86-year-old poet Robert Frost, an earnest of the cultural ambitions of the new occupants of the White House. In the primary and presidential campaigns Jack had often rounded off a speech with a geographically appropriate paraphrase of a Frost poem:

> *Iowa City is lovely, dark and deep*
> *But I have promises to keep*
> *And miles to go before I sleep*

For the inauguration Frost had written a few lines of Laureate-like doggerel, but blinded by sun on winter snow, he recited from memory an earlier poem, *The Gift Outright.*

At 12.51 the oath was administered by Chief Justice Earl Warren. Then Kennedy stepped forward to deliver an inaugural address which electrified all those who heard it and reverberated around the world.

He had been working on it since the election. Suggestions had been solicited from the great and the good by Ted Sorensen, and a mass of helpful advice had poured in, including selected Biblical quotes from Billy Graham and Isaac Frank, director of the Jewish Community Council in Washington, neither of them, as Henry Fairlie observed, "the most obvious sources to which one would expect a Roman Catholic to look for scriptural inspiration".

The guiding hand, as ever, was provided by Ted Sorensen, the meticulous technician of Jack's rhetoric. The most important decision, taken on 16 January, was to confine the address to foreign affairs, with only a single oblique reference to the domestic issue of civil rights. The finishing touches were applied on the eve of the inauguration. Flying from Palm Beach to Washington on *Caroline*, Jack slipped

Opposite: The oath of office is administered by Chief Justice Warren. In the bitterly cold weather JFK then spoke without a coat.

the final draft into a drawer with the wry remark that "An early draft of Roosevelt's Inaugural was discovered the other day and brought $200,000 at an auction".

The speech was in turn brilliant, moving and, seen with the advantage of hindsight, dangerous. It called upon Americans as heirs to their own revolutionary traditions to undertake a new global mission: "Let the word go forth from this time and place, to friend and foe alike, that the torch has been passed to a new generation of Americans – born in this century, tempered by war, disciplined by a hard and bitter peace, proud of our ancient heritage and unwilling to witness or permit the slow undoing of those human rights to which this nation has always been committed and to which we are committed today at home and around the world."

No limits were set on this mission: "Let every nation know, whether it wishes us well or ill, that we shall pay any price, bear any burden, meet any hardship, support any friend, oppose any foe, in order to assure the survival and success of liberty. This much we pledge – and more."

The accomplishment of the mission required collective and individual sacrifice. Evoking the "voluntary totalitarianism" of *Why England Slept*, Kennedy crystallized the message toward which he had been moving in many of his campaign speeches: "And so, my fellow Americans, ask not what your country can do for you; ask what you can do for your country."

Leaving the ceremony, Sam Rayburn, the bald Bourbon-guzzling Speaker of the House of Representatives, declared: "That speech he made over there was better than anything Franklin Roosevelt said at his best – it was better than Lincoln. I think – really think – that he's a man of destiny." Later Carl Sandberg wrote of the speech, "Around nearly every sentence of it could be written a thesis, so packed is it with implications." But what would happen when the implications found concrete expressions in policy?

Eisenhower had seen himself as a president above party and faction, akin to a benevolent monarch who ran the executive branch by the same rules of order and hierarchy he had employed during his distinguished military career, while leaving the legislature a relatively free hand in framing financial and legislative policy. Tolerant and moderate, he was reluctant to exploit the full resources of the presidency, except at election times.

His successor at the White House was seized with a highly romantic view of the office. Jack Kennedy's was to be a personal presidency in which the collective energy of the nation would be galvanized by his leadership. He had made his intentions clear while campaigning, asserting that "the American people elect a President to act". Ike had attracted criticism for not using the full powers of the office, but Jack Kennedy had no such inhibitions. At the beginning of his presidential campaign, he told the National Press Club in Washington that the president must, above all, be "the Chief Executive, in every sense of the

Above: One of the features of his inaugural parade which delighted Jack Kennedy most was a PT-boat in the markings of his old command manned for the day by his former shipmates. Right: Listening to the most striking inaugural speech since that delivered by Franklin Delano Roosevelt in 1932: immediately behind JFK, Lyndon Johnson and Richard Nixon; two rows back wearing homburg, Richard Cardinal Cushing; and on far right of front row, Senator John Sparkman of Alabama and former president Harry S. Truman.

word. He must be prepared to exercise the fullest powers of his office – all that are specified and some that are not."

Much influenced by the exalted view of the presidency painted in Richard E. Neustadt's fashionable book *Presidential Power*, Kennedy saw himself as a streamlined version of Franklin Delano Roosevelt, recapturing for the office the power and the élan which Eisenhower had yielded to his Cabinet and to the cautious bureaucratic tyranny of committees. And in so doing he would emulate FDR as the actor-manager of his own political drama, not only enjoying the exercise of power but being seen to do so. By sheer force of personality, he would make the grim and impersonal world of power something

personal, not only for his fellow countrymen but also for all the peoples around the world.

This contrasts sharply with the circumspection of Jack's early political career, in which little was left to chance or hostage to fortune. But it set the tone of his presidency and generated a new set of myths around the assembling of his administration.

From the moment of his election Kennedy's "great talent hunt" had whipped up a frenzy of excitement in the press which suggested that no one had ever formed an administration before. Washington crackled with expectation, prompting *Time* to comment sourly of the administration-in-waiting, "Sometimes they almost sound as if they had invented the town."

The excitement masked the fact that many

of Kennedy's appointments were entirely conventional. The political establishment was unlikely to be ruffled by the retention of Eisenhower's Under Secretary of State for Economic Affairs, Douglas Dillon, as Treasury Secretary; or the appointment of the Republican President of the Rockefeller Foundation, Dean Rusk, as Secretary of State. There was a sharp intake of breath among liberals when it was announced that J. Edgar Hoover was to remain at the FBI and Allen W. Dulles was to continue as director of the CIA. Those whom Jack considered "doctrinaire liberals", such as J.K. Galbraith, were kept well away from the levers of power. More controversial was Jack's appointment of Robert Kennedy as his Attorney-General, a logical move given the intimate political relationship which had developed between the brothers, but one which was bound to attract accusations of nepotism. Anticipating the furore, not least because his brother had never practised law, Jack jokingly suggested that Bobby's appointment should be announced to an empty street at two in the morning. One unstated reason for Bobby's appointment was Jack's pressing need to "handle" J. Edgar Hoover with the utmost caution and confidentiality, something which could only be accomplished with his brother heading the Justice Department.

Of all those who came to Washington to serve Jack Kennedy it was the Praetorian Guard of brilliant academics and technicians, "the best and the brightest", who lent the administration its particular flavor and a brief luster which was to tarnish by the end of the decade. These were Jack Kennedy's outriders of American empire. The junior officers of the Second World War, they were now entering their Cold War inheritance, for it was in foreign affairs that their influence was to be felt. Like the earlier imperial cadres celebrated by John Buchan, they prided themselves on their cool in crisis, laconic wit and ability to move easily between the worlds of thought and action. They were variously described as "tough", "hardnosed" and "pragmatic".

Three archetypal examples of the New Frontiersman were McGeorge Bundy, Walt W. Rostow and Robert McNamara. Bundy came from Harvard University to serve Kennedy as Assistant Secretary of Defense for National Security Affairs. His first task in the new adminstration had been to perform radical surgery on the elaborate security apparatus bequeathed by Eisenhower, reducing it, in Arthur Schlesinger's words, to "a supple instrument to meet the President's distinctive needs".

In the Second World War, as aide to Vice-Admiral Kirk, Bundy had been closely involved in the planning for D-Day. Ferociously hard-working with a tight, frosty smile and an equally chilly way with those he considered his intellectual inferiors, Bundy reinforced his formidable intellectual reputation with a genius for administration, the "clerk of the world" as he was dubbed by one disillusioned subordinate.

The largest of the inaugural balls, held at the Washington Armory. The President and the first lady watch as members of the Cabinet and their wives are introduced. Jackie wore a stunning Oleg Cassini gown of white chiffon, covered with a floor-length silk cape.

Left: A meeting held in JFK's Hyannis Port living room in 1961 to discuss the defense and science budgets. Clockwise from the left: General Lyman L. Lemnitzer, Chairman of the Joint Chiefs, Special Military Assistant Maxwell Taylor (who later became Chairman of the Joint Chiefs), Secretary of Defense Robert McNamara, the President, Director of the Budget David Bell, Deputy Secretary of Defense Roswell Gilpatric, Scientific Adviser Jerome Wiesner. Opposite: New Frontiersmen. JFK with Robert McNamara (left) and Secretary of State Dean Rusk. The President is relaxing in one of the padded rocking chairs he used to ease his painful back.

Bundy's deputy was Walt Rostow, an economic historian from the Massachusetts Institute of Technology. Rostow's wartime career had been spent picking bombing targets for the USAAF and he remained an unrepentant believer in the power of the strategic bomber long after its limitations had been exposed. Rostow was the think tank man par excellence, bursting with ideas for every conceivable scenario, a combination of intellectual arrogance and naivety. It was a mark of Rostow's and Bundy's supreme self-confidence, amounting to hubris, that they divided the world between them, Bundy taking everything west of Suez and Rostow assuming responsibility for everything to the east.

Kennedy's Defense Secretary Robert McNamara was the most important of the three men. Like Bundy a Republican, he had been part of the brilliant young team assembled by Robert Lovett to apply systems analysis to the massive wartime expansion of the American air force. After the war he was one of the legendary "whiz kids" who rescued the ailing Ford Motor Company, becoming its president at the same time as Jack Kennedy assumed office.

McNamara's slicked-down helmet of hair and daunting rimless glasses were tokens of his relentless drive, making him the high-priest of the can-do brotherhood. He was the intellectual-as-manager – he read Teilhard de

Chardin in his spare time – who would assert civilian control over a Pentagon wedded to the brute instruments of massive retaliation. In the Kennedy administration McNamara occupied a more influential position than the unobtrusive Rusk, who was happy to describe himself as looking like a "neighborhood bartender", and who always seemed slightly ill at ease among the jostling, nakedly ambitious thrusters of the New Frontier.

Charts, statistics, data of all kinds were meat and drink to these men. They had a fierce belief that the intractable problems of the Third World would yield to the gathering of intelligence and the application of rational analysis. Like precision tools on the production line, their intellectual hardware would manipulate problems at home and abroad and reshape the map of the world. They soon discovered that the real and imprecise nature of Third World politics did not respond readily to these methods. The intellectual elite of the New Frontier was to suffer a long and agonizing disillusionment.

The New Frontiersmen shared with their President a fascination with guerrilla warfare and counterinsurgency. Assigned to numerous "task forces", they were launched on a kind of guerrilla war against the Washington bureaucracy, particularly that of the State Department. Jack Kennedy wanted to be his own Secretary of State - hence the appointment of Rusk, "everyone's Number Two" – and to foster a decision-making process which ran outside "normal channels",

Opposite: Affairs of state. The President and Defense Secretary Robert McNamara in the White House rose garden. McNamara's confidence that the problems of the Third World would yield to the application of business methods and rational analysis was to be undermined in the years following Kennedy's assassination. Right: Smiling through. JFK's abundant natural charm survived the severest crises of his presidency. The replica of George Washington's sword which hangs behind him serves as a visual metaphor for the nuclear sword of Damocles which hung over his presidency.

reproducing the "creative chaos" of the Kennedy family. Just as the Kennedy children had competed for the ambassador's attention, so the "best and the brightest" would jockey for access to and influence on the President.

Memories of the Kennedy mania for competition were stirred when a few weeks into Jack's presidency McGeorge Bundy used a sporting metaphor to describe the new administration, "At this point we are like the Harlem Globetrotters, passing forward, behind, sideways and underneath. But nobody has made a basket yet." But the Cold War equivalent of the Victorian "Great Game" was about to begin.

From the outset Jack Kennedy concentrated on foreign policy. "Domestic policy," he observed, "can only defeat us; foreign policy can kill us." Hammering out his Cold War credentials during the presidential campaign, he had warned the American people that the next decade would be "a hazardous experience. We will live on the edge of danger". In the State of the Union message he delivered a week after taking office, he repeated the warning: "Before my term has ended we shall have to test whether a nation organized as our own can endure ... Each day the crises multiply. Each day the solution becomes more difficult. Each day we draw nearer to the hour of maximum danger."

This apocalyptic imagery came easily to a young president who had courted death since childhood and had cast himself as the romantic lead in the global psychodrama of

the Cold War. But for the American people, twelve million of whom would soon invest in their own backyard fallout shelters, the diet of permanent crisis on which the White House initially thrived was to prove a taxing and sometimes alarming regime. Jack Kennedy wanted to pull the nation up on to tiptoe, but such a posture can only be maintained for so long.

The Kennedy administration was committed not merely to the containment of Communism but to moving forward to meet and challenge it on ground of its own choosing. The Peace Corps and the Latin American Alliance for Progress were diplomatic manifestations of this policy; the military manifestation was reflected in a rapid build-up of both conventional and nuclear forces. In this global contest, where freedom and Communism were "locked in a deadly embrace", there would always be a forward point of confrontation where the clock stood at one minute to midnight.

The Soviet leader Nikita Khrushchev had thrown down the gauntlet barely a fortnight before Kennedy's inauguration, with a speech in which he claimed that imperialism would be brought low by Third World wars of national liberation. Among the centers of "revolutionary struggle against imperialism" he cited were Algeria, Vietnam and Cuba.

In the 1960 campaign Jack Kennedy had indulged in some heavy saber rattling against Fidel Castro's Marxist regime in Cuba. However, the repeated charges of feebleness

The President disappears in a blizzard of tickertape in Mexico City in July 1962. Latin America was the focus of his "Alliance for Progress", an aid program aimed at underpinning Latin American economic development and bolstering democracy in the region. Behind the idealism lay the aim of stopping the spread of Marxism. Kennedy believed that the Alliance would "counter the Communist onslaught in this hemisphere".

over this bone in the American throat which he leveled at the Eisenhower administration were somewhat disingenous, as he had been briefed about current operations aimed at the removal of Castro. Overseen by Vice-President Richard Nixon and under the direction of Richard Bissell, the Deputy Director of Plans at the CIA, a covert campaign against Castro had been devised which Jack Kennedy inherited full-blown.

The CIA had dreamed up a number of absurd ideas to dispose of Castro, including a plan to dust his shoes with a depilatory which would, at a stroke, remove his beard and his machismo. More sinister was the recruitment of a number Mafia bosses – who had controlled Cuba's casinos and vice rings in the days of the Batista dictatorship – to assist in the assassination of Castro. Among the mobsters who were enlisted in this program was Sam Giancana.

During 1960 the CIA had scoured the expatriate anti-Castro Cuban underground in Miami, recruiting some 1,500 men, who were formed into Brigade 2506 and sent to training camps in Guatemala to prepare for an attack on Cuba which, it was hoped, would spark a general uprising against Castro. Cuban pilots were trained to fly obsolete USAF B-26 bombers from an airstrip in Nicaragua to support Brigade 2506's landings on Cuba. It was intended to pass them off as disaffected Cubans who had defected with their aircraft.

The $13 million budget for the plan had been approved with the proviso that no US personnel were to be involved in the front line. However, by the time Kennedy took office Bissell's jealously guarded plans were beginning to cause grave misgivings among senior officers in the US armed forces and in the CIA itself. Nevertheless, on the day before his inauguration Kennedy was told by Eisenhower that the project was going well and that the new president had the "responsibility" to do "whatever is necessary" to ensure its success.

Kennedy now faced a dilemma. The operation had acquired a momentum of its own, but leaks to the press had already occurred and the existence of the plan was common knowledge in the Cuban expatriate community in Miami. Abandonment of the plan would expose the administration to accusations of cowardice and would also create a considerable problem over the "disposal" of the force training in Guatemala. Kennedy hesitated, but his resolve to continue was undoubtedly strengthened by the ambassador, who urged him to press on. He was also reassured by Allen Dulles, who reminded him of the success of the CIA-backed 1954 coup in Guatemala, which had removed the Arbenz government and had been masterminded by Richard Bissell. The clinching factors were Kennedy's fascination with covert operations – one facet of the "flexible response" he had proposed to counter Communist aggression – and his high regard for Bissell, another tough-talking intellectual, who had developed the U-2 spy plane program and described himself as the president's "man-eating shark".

Kennedy was determined that the operation should make as little "noise" as possible. On 12 April he announced at a press conference that "there will not be, under any conditions, an intervention in Cuba by United States armed forces". US involvement had to be "deniable". Kennedy was prepared to provide the invasion fleet with an escort of five destroyers and the aircraft carrier Essex, but he stipulated that no US forces were to take any aggressive action. The original choice of landing site, at Trinidad near the Escambray Mountains, was changed to the more remote Bahia de Cochinos, the Bay of Pigs, which was surrounded by swamps and some 80 miles from sheltering mountains if the landings went awry.

Kennedy did not enjoy unanimous support for the operation within the administration. Dean Rusk, Arthur Schlesinger, the president's special assistant, and Under Secretary of State Chester Bowles all argued against the plan, but their voices were never likely to be decisive. Senator J. William Fulbright, who knew about the plans in spite of their supposed secrecy, sent a cogent memorandum to the president warning of the dangers of intervention in Cuba. Invited to attend a Cabinet meeting on 4 April, Fulbright argued that if the operation went ahead the United States would be faced with the choice of letting it fail (if, as Fulbright believed, Brigade 2506 was rapidly

isolated) or of supporting it with greater military assistance. To follow the second course would not only reveal the United States as no better than the Soviet Union but would also force the administration into an open-ended commitment to maintaining stability in Cuba.

Fulbright was politely heard out but the operation went ahead. Sensing the growing apprehension on all sides, Kennedy remarked, "everybody's grabbing their nuts on this one". He reduced the air component so that only six B-26 bombers with no defensive armament were tasked with the destruction of the Cuban air force as a preliminary to the landings. They failed, their abortive mission ensuring that Castro's forces were fully alerted when the landings were made in the small hours of 17 April. The beach-head was swiftly sealed off by Cuban armor, while the Cuban air force sank Brigade 2506's two supply ships and with them three-quarters of the invasion force's ammunition.

The operation was rapidly unraveling. The American press had quickly seen through the amateurish fiction of a Cuban "defector" who had landed a battle-damaged aircraft with Cuban markings in Florida. He was identified as a member of the Cuban exile community, causing deep embarrassment to the US ambassador to the United Nations, Adlai Stevenson, who had innocently been using the incident to deny charges of American involvement. Meanwhile, the members of the Cuban provisional government in exile, waiting to be flown in triumph to Cuba by the CIA, were now proving so difficult to handle that they had to be held incommunicado. As Castro rolled up Brigade 2506's beach-head, Kennedy came under great pressure to cover the evacuation with US aircraft. Finally he sanctioned a sortie by six unmarked jets from Essex to escort B-26s flown from Nicaragua. Even then the jets were ordered to fire only in defense of the bombers. The jets missed their rendezvous and the B-26s were shot down.

As the operation collapsed around his ears Kennedy attempted to maintain the appearance of normality. On the night of 18 April he arrived, smiling and relaxed, and arm-in-arm with Jackie, at the annual Congressional reception in the White House. The band played *Mr Wonderful* as the couple made their entrance. Two hours later, still in white tie and tails, he was deep in a crisis meeting in the Oval Office, where the "man-eating shark", now haggard and unshaven, cataloged the unfolding disaster. By 20 April it was all over. Castro's forces had captured 1,150 men of Brigade 2506, and only 150 had been taken off the beach-head by US Navy personnel wearing T-shirts. Bissell's and Allen Dulles' days were numbered and within a few months both had resigned.

Meetings followed with Eisenhower and Nixon, both of whom took a bi-partisan approach to the debacle. Nixon, the "father" of the operation, later recalled: "[Kennedy] jumped up from his chair and began pacing back and forth in front of his desk. His anger

and frustration poured out in a profane barrage... 'I was assured by every son of a bitch I checked with – all the military experts and the CIA – that the plan would succeed...' Everything had been going so well for him; a few days earlier he had stood high in the polls, and his press was overwhelmingly favorable. Now he was in deep trouble, and he felt he was the innocent victim of bad advice from men whom he trusted ... It suddenly struck me how alone he must feel – how wronged yet how responsible.... [It] was not entirely his fault but nonetheless his inescapable responsibility."

Kennedy assumed responsibility for the debacle at a press conference shortly afterward: "There's an old saying that victory has a hundred fathers and defeat is an orphan. I'm the responsible officer of the government." He also confided to Ted Sorensen, "How could I have been so far off base? All my life I've known better than to depend on the experts. How could I have been so stupid to let them go ahead?" Many years later Chester Bowles wrote in his memoirs: "The humiliating failure of the invasion shattered the myth of a New Frontier run by a new breed of incisive fault-free supermen. However costly, it may have been a necessary lesson."

The Bay of Pigs did little to dent Jack Kennedy's high standing in the polls nor did it bring down the curtain on covert operations against Cuba. While an inquest was held on the Bay of Pigs – focusing on tactical

Recollection, but little tranquility – JFK confers with former President Eisenhower after the disastrous Bay of Pigs operation. Later Eisenhower expressed the opinion that, at this early stage in his presidency, Kennedy regarded the office as "not only a very personal thing, but as an institution that one man could handle with an assistant here and another there. He had no idea of the complexity of the job". But the fact remains that the original plan was Ike's.

Left: In December 1962 the President and the first lady reviewed the veterans of the Bay of Pigs operation in Miami. The 40,000-strong crowd applauded a short speech Jackie gave in Spanish praising the courage of the Cuban exiles. Presented with a rebel flag, JFK assured his audience that " ... this flag will will be returned to this brigade on Cuban soil". Opposite: JFK and Jackie with President de Gaulle at Versailles, 2 June 1961, on their way to the Hall of Mirrors for a glittering state dinner. Jackie, dressed by Givenchy, made a great hit with the French public, prompting Jack to tell the press, "I am the man who accompanied Jacqueline Kennedy to Paris, and I have enjoyed it."

shortcomings rather than on the sheer fantasy which underlay the entire operation – a new covert campaign to harass Castro, Operation Mongoose, was set in place under the direction of counterinsurgency expert General Edward Lansdale. Bobby Kennedy, who had not been closely involved in the Bay of Pigs operation, was the driving force behind Operation Mongoose, which was to absorb tens of millions of dollars in economic sabotage and the promotion of harebrained schemes to destroy the Cuban regime, including the assassination of Castro. George Ball, who as Under Secretary of State was involved in reviewing these covert operations, recalled: "Most of them, in my view, were either absurd or just plain childish. Some were recklessly dangerous ... They were based on the improbable assumption that, given money or encouragement, the population of a whole country would rise against its leader. America's objective, as they described it, was to achieve democracy by replacing 'their bastard with our bastard'."

The failure of the Bay of Pigs operation had left Jack Kennedy exposed when he met Nikita Khrushchev in Vienna in June 1961. Kennedy arrived in Vienna after a state visit to France, where public enthusiasm for the handsome young President and his beautiful wife was tempered by President de Gaulle's stern warning that any American military intervention in Vietnam would condemn the United States to sinking "step by step into a

bottomless military and political quagmire, however much you spend in men and money".

De Gaulle had reservations about Kennedy's youth and inexperience. Khrushchev believed that it could be exploited and that he could dominate Kennedy in a head-to-head confrontation. For Jack the meeting offered him the chance to recover his poise and to prove that he was as tough as the rumbustious Khrushchev.

The talks did not go well. In considerable pain from a strained back and possibly suffering from mild disorientation induced by the cocktail of drugs injected daily to ease his pain by Dr Max Jacobson, the showbusiness charlatan known as "Dr Feelgood", Kennedy made heavy weather of his personal diplomacy with Khrushchev. He made a schoolboyish attempt to debate Khrushchev on Marxism, a subject of which Jack had only the most superficial knowledge, and at least twice had to endure the Soviet leader's calculated tantrums: first when he suggested that a Soviet "miscalculation" might trigger a nuclear exchange; and in the final session when Khrushchev threatened to start such an

Above: A contrast in styles – Jackie, the essence of chic, and the homely Mrs Khrushchev. The Soviet premier doted on Jackie, paying her special attention at the official dinner and plying her with earthy anecdotes. Opposite: JFK with Nikita Khrushchev at their summit meeting in Vienna in June 1961. It was a stormy first encounter, but their relationship matured into one of considerable mutual sympathy and understanding.

exchange over Berlin.

Kennedy came away from the Vienna summit in somber mood. In London, Prime Minister Macmillan found him "rather stunned" – baffled might perhaps have been fairer – by the mauling he had received at Khrushchev's hands. He later told Lem Billings that dealing with Khrushchev was rather like handling his father – "all take and no give". Above all, the summit had underlined the critical importance of the divided city of Berlin, the focus of Cold War tensions and the potential flash point for nuclear war.

At Vienna Khrushchev had threatened to sign a separate peace treaty with East Germany, which would enable the Soviet Union to control access to Berlin and render the position of the NATO forces in the city untenable. Within a month of the summit he had made six major speeches in which he raised the question of Berlin. In July he announced a 25 per cent increase in military spending. Kennedy called for a similar expansion of the US military budget and on 25 July responded with a television speech in which he described Berlin as the "great testing place of Western courage and will, a focal point where our solemn commitment, stretching back over the years since 1945, and Soviet ambitions now meet in basic confrontation".

The Soviet Union was now under increasing pressure to cut off Berlin as the migration of East Germany's "best and brightest" to the West continued unabated. Threatened with

losing its entire technical and managerial elite, and facing a growing industrial and agricultural crisis, the decision was taken to staunch the flow, and on 13 August the construction of the Berlin Wall began.

West Berlin's Mayor Willy Brandt requested immediate help from Kennedy and some Bonn students sent the President a black umbrella, symbol of Neville Chamberlain's policy of appeasement. Kennedy held back from precipitate action, sending Vice-President Johnson on a mission to Berlin accompanied by General Lucius D. Clay, hero of the Berlin airlift of 1948-9. At the same time the US Army was ordered to push a 1,500-man battle group down the autobahn to Berlin. It arrived without mishap the day after Johnson had reassured West Berliners that "We are with you in the determination to defend your liberty and the holy cause of human freedom". Clay remained in Berlin as the President's special representative.

Behind the pious clichés there lurked a measure of realpolitik. Although he could never admit it publicly, Kennedy was privately relieved at the outcome of the Berlin crisis. The building of the Wall would, in the long term, relieve pressure in Berlin rather than exacerbate it. The ending of the exodus to the West meant that there would in all probability be no new crisis over Berlin. In October there was a brief, ugly confrontation of tanks across Checkpoint Charlie, but access to West Berlin remained open and the Soviet treaty with East Germany remained unsigned.

Left: JFK with the British Prime Minister Harold Macmillan, with whom he enjoyed a particularly close relationship. Their friendship sometimes clouded the President's judgement about British economic and military weakness when compared with American strength. On one famous occasion Jack confided in Macmillan that if he did not have sex every day he got a headache. Macmillan's reply is not recorded.

Opposite: JFK with Willy Brandt, then Mayor of West Berlin, at the Brandenburg Gate in Berlin in June 1963. The East Berlin authorities covered the arches with red cloth to prevent the President from seeing into East Berlin.

However, when Jack Kennedy saw the reality of the Wall on his triumphant visit to West Berlin in June 1963, at a time when he was moving toward a détente with the Soviet Union, his Cold War instincts were aroused. Just as he had been stirred to eloquence by the poverty he had seen in West Virginia during the 1960 primaries, so he was now moved to deliver in the Rudolf Wilde Platz the speech in which he declared: "All free men, wherever they may live, are citizens of Berlin, and therefore, as a free man, I take pride in the words 'Ich bin ein Berliner'."

George Ball observed of the Cold War that "a continuing tension between two major military powers is like a high fever. It may have to reach a crisis before it can subside." In the relentless jockeying between the United States and the Soviet Union the "hour of maximum danger" which Jack Kennedy had predicted arrived with the start of the Cuban missile crisis.

Operation Mongoose had driven Fidel Castro to request increased military aid from

the Soviet Union. In Nikita Khrushchev he found a willing supplier, and throughout the early months of 1962 surface-to-air missiles (SAMs), nuclear-capable bombers, MiG fighters, tanks, artillery, small arms and thousands of Soviet troops poured into Cuba, partly to bolster Castro against the threat of American invasion but also to test the resolve of the White House.

The Kennedy administration chose to ignore the build-up while it consisted of essentially defensive weaponry and offered no direct threat to US interests. However, by August 1962 the scale of Soviet military activity on Cuba had convinced Dulles' successor as Director of the CIA, John McCone, that preparations were being made to install long-range missiles which would threaten the United States mainland.

At first Kennedy was not inclined to take McCone's suspicions seriously, but they were dramatically confirmed on 15 October when a U-2 reconnaissance aircraft flying a high-level sweep over military sites to the west of Havana returned with incontrovertible evidence that Soviet technicians were preparing sites for nuclear-capable medium-range ballistic missiles (MRBMs). Within a week there was evidence of work on more missile sites which would bring the entire mainland of the United States under threat. The presence of missiles on Cuba was confirmed but not that of nuclear warheads. (In 1989 the Soviets revealed that warheads were in place and the missiles could have been armed and operational within two hours.)

The Soviets had placed missiles in Cuba as a short cut to achieving nuclear parity with the United States. When John Kennedy became President he jokingly asked Robert McNamara, "Whoever believed in the 'missile gap' anyway?" The right answer would have been the Soviet Union. In reality there had always been a "missile gap", but it was one which operated in favor of the United States, which by 1961 enjoyed a superiority in warheads of 5,000 to 300, a 3-1 advantage in strategic bombers and a 6-1 advantage in intercontinental ballistic missiles (ICBMs). Research and development to produce more powerful and accurate Soviet missiles was underway, but accelerating it to match the US program would have imposed intolerable strains on the creaking Soviet economy. Under heavy pressure from hardliners in the Soviet military, Khrushchev seized on the alternative, moving medium-range missiles to within 100 miles of the United States.

As Robert McNamara pointed out to Jack Kennedy at the beginning of the crisis, the missiles in Cuba had no appreciable effect on the overall balance of power. But it was equally clear that knowledge of their presence would have a seismic effect on American public opinion. Shielded by the Atlantic and Pacific Oceans, the American mainland had been unscathed by two world wars. The American public was now making the painful readjustment to being targeted by Soviet ICBMs, but the reality of this threat was

The President delivers his famous West Berlin speech on 24 June 1963, telling a wildly enthusiastic crowd that in the free world the proudest boast was "Ich bin ein Berliner", a short phrase which apparently took him an age to memorize. It has gained an extra resonance with the fall of the Berlin Wall.

Opposite: JFK receives Soviet Deputy Foreign Minister Sermonov (left), Ambassador Dobrynin and Foreign Minister Gromyko in the Oval Office on 18 October 1963. The smiles are forced. It was too early for JFK to show his hand about the missiles, although the photographs were in a drawer in his desk. Given every opportunity to admit the missiles' presence on Cuba, Gromyko merely stonewalled. Right: The photograph of the missile site at San Cristobal, Cuba, which was shown to the President early on the morning of 16 October 1963. It had been taken by a U-2 reconnaissance aircraft piloted by Major Rudolf Anderson, USAF. On 27 October Anderson was shot down and killed on another mission over Cuba.

tempered by the missiles' distance from the United States. The prospect of missiles in Cuba would be psychologically insupportable and a challenge to the Monroe Doctrine, which would not countenance any European meddling in the Western hemisphere.

Jack Kennedy was informed of the U-2's discovery when he was woken at 8am on 16 October. He immediately set up an ad hoc group of advisers which became known as the Executive Committee of the National Security Council or ExComm. A combination of trusted colleagues and Cold War hardliners, ExComm included Bobby Kennedy, Dean Rusk, John McCone, McGeorge Bundy, Robert McNamara and General Maxwell Taylor, the Chairman of the Joint Chiefs of Staff. For the next two weeks ExComm was in almost continuous session, for the most part in George Ball's conference room at the State Department. The President maintained his normal routine to avoid alerting the press, fortuitously distracted by the November elections, while Bobby Kennedy acted as the link between the President and ExComm. This freewheeling breach of policy-making procedure alarmed the former Secretary of State Dean Acheson, who was one of a shifting cast of experts who sat in on ExComm's deliberations. On 20 October, however, the situation had become sufficiently grave for the President to cut short a visit to Chicago and return to Washington. The press was told that he was "suffering from a head cold".

ExComm debated the American response for six days. The advocates of a purely diplomatic approach quickly fell by the wayside and argument moved on to the options favored by the US military. The Joint Chiefs of Staff urged a full-scale invasion of Cuba, which would almost certainly have been the prelude to the Third World War. Setting this sobering option aside, ExComm narrowed the focus of its discussions to the launching of a "surgical" air strike against the missile sites or the imposition of a maritime blockade of Cuba to cut Castro off from his Soviet quartermasters.

No one could guarantee the complete success of an air strike, which would cause heavy casualties among civilians and Soviet personnel and might leave missiles intact to be fired at the United States. George Ball had a healthy suspicion of the advocates of air power: "I had been a director of the United States Strategic Bombing Survey at the end of the Second World War and had concluded from the record of Allied bombing in Europe that if the medical profession should ever adopt the air force definition of 'surgical', anyone undergoing an operation for appendicitis might lose his kidneys and lungs yet find his appendix intact."

During ExComm's deliberations, Bobby Kennedy in particular had argued forcefully against an air strike. The President, now under mounting strain, was also alarmed by the risks inherent in such a course of action. After enduring a hectoring hymn to the glories of bombing delivered by General Curtis Le May, the USAF's Chief of Staff, the President was

reduced to a state of rage; according to Roswell Gilpatric, the Deputy Secretary of Defense, the President was "just beside himself, as close as he ever got".

A blockade on the other hand, would be difficult to organize and impose and, as an act of war, might be a breach of international law. Nor would it do anything about the missiles on Cuba. But it would give the Soviet Union time to consider its own options. Meanwhile photo-reconnaissance continued to chart steady progress on the construction of the missile sites. On 22 October, having placed American nuclear forces on full alert, Jack Kennedy went on nationwide television, informing the American public for the first time of the gravity of the crisis and reminding them of recent history: " The 1930s taught us a clear lesson: aggressive conduct, if allowed to go unchecked and unchallenged, ultimately leads to war." He outlined the options available to the administration and then announced his chosen course of action. If the Soviets did not begin to dismantle the missile sites and halt the arms build-up by 10am on 24 October, a "quarantine line" of US Navy vessels would be placed around Cuba. They would stop, search and, if necessary, turn back any Soviet or Soviet-chartered ship crossing the line.

At least twenty-five Soviet-controlled ships were known to be steaming toward Cuba. Simultaneously the seventeen destroyers and two cruisers of Admiral Alfred Ward's Task Force 136 were already maneuvering to cut off Cuba from its eastern approaches. In Florida

The President at work at his desk in the Oval Office. Appropriately for a seafaring man, the desk was fashioned from the timbers of a 19th-century British warship, Resolute. *The desk was presented to President Hayes by Queen Victoria in 1878. JFK is surrounded by personal memorabilia, including the coconut on which he wrote his famous message in 1943. The scrambler buttons are clearly visible on the telephone console. Opposite: A brief moment of calm with Bobby.*

and the Gulf ports, the US Navy was secretly readying a massive force for the invasion of Cuba, comprising some 25,000 Marines aboard Navy vessels supported by 100,000 Army troops. In a personal letter to Khrushchev, Kennedy stressed the United States' determination and reflected on the insanity of nuclear war in which " it is crystal clear no country could win and which would only result in catastrophic consequences to the whole world, including the aggressor".

It had now been made clear to Khrushchev that the blockade was merely the first in a series of controlled steps leading to nuclear war. On the diplomatic front, Kennedy received support from the Organization of American States and his NATO allies. At the United Nations Adlai Stevenson, always considered something of a wimp by Kennedy, scored a personal triumph, combatively producing copies of the U-2 photographs to expose Soviet dissimulation over the missile sites.

But it was on the high seas that the matter would be decided. By the morning of 24 October there were 63 ships, including some from Latin American countries, on the quarantine line. In the White House as the hands of the clock passed 10am, Robert McNamara announced that two of the Soviet ships were now only a few miles from the quarantine line, 500 miles off the coast of Cuba. An interception would be made before noon. Then a report came in that a Soviet submarine had been sighted between the two ships. The aircraft carrier Essex was standing by to force the submarine to surface and identify itself, using depth charges if necessary. Bobby Kennedy later recalled his brother's reaction as the tension mounted: "His hand went up to his face and covered his mouth. He opened and closed his fist. His face seemed drawn, his eyes pained, almost gray. We stared at each other across the table ..."

At 10.25am a preliminary report arrived indicating that some of the Soviet ships had stopped dead in the water. Several minutes later it was confirmed that six ships on the edge of the quarantine line had stopped or were turning back. Dean Rusk commented, "We're eyeball to eyeball and I think the other fellow just blinked."

This news provided only temporary respite. On 25 October, the Soviet ships resumed their passage westward. At 7am on the 26th, in an act rich with symbolism, the *Marucla*, a Soviet-chartered freighter, was boarded inside the quarantine zone by sailors from the destroyer *Joseph P. Kennedy Jr*. A search revealed no proscribed materiel and the *Marucla* sailed on.

Kennedy was still toying with the idea of an invasion, but now cracks were beginning to appear in the Soviet position. As the day wore on, the Soviets used a back-channel to present a face-saving formula in which Khrushchev would agree to dismantle the missile sites in return for an American pledge not to invade Cuba. That evening Kennedy received a verbose and emotional letter from the Soviet leader. While continuing to protest that the missiles had been

installed solely to prevent American aggression, it confirmed the terms offered earlier in the day and allowed Khrushchev to join Kennedy in his apprehension about nuclear war, which he said could only be started by "lunatics or suicides, who themselves want to perish and to destroy the whole world before they die".

Again the crisis threatened to spin out of control. On the 27th a second, and more formal Soviet message arrived, curtly linking the withdrawal of the missiles with American removal of Jupiter missiles from Turkey. It is likely that the first had been drafted by Khrushchev personally; the second came from the Kremlin hardliners. News also came in of two U-2 incidents: in the first a U-2 had been shot down over Cuba and the pilot killed; in the second another U-2 on a routine air-testing flight over the North Pole had briefly strayed into Soviet airspace, causing Robert McNamara to exclaim, "This means war with the Soviet Union."

As the members of ExComm approached a state of exhaustion, conveyed vividly by transcripts of tapes of the meetings on the 27th, the threat of nuclear war receded. Bobby Kennedy broke the logjam by suggesting that they simply ignore the second Soviet communication and act on the first. The gamble paid off. On the morning of 28 October the Kremlin agreed to withdraw the missiles from Cuba in return for American assurances that there would be no invasion of Cuba. As the tension broke, Kennedy told Arthur Schlesinger, in an aside which history has given

a terrible irony, "This is the night to go to the theater, like Abraham Lincoln."

In a secret meeting with the Soviet ambassador Anatoly Dobrynin, Bobby Kennedy conveyed in guarded language an additional assurance that the Jupiter missiles in Turkey would be removed. The correspondence between Khrushchev and Kennedy released in January 1992 reveals that the latter attached a number of conditions to his assurances on the invasion of Cuba, including the stipulation that "Cuba itself commits no aggression against any of the nations of the Western hemisphere". Operation Mongoose was wound up, but covert operations against Castro continued, albeit on a reduced scale.

A widely held view of Kennedy's handling of the missile crisis is that it provides striking proof of his ability to grow into the burdensome office of the presidency. Harold Macmillan, with whom Kennedy kept in touch all through the crisis, thought that he had displayed "extraordinary skill", playing "a firm military game throughout – acting quickly and being ready to act as soon as mobilized". The commentator James Reston has written: "He was tested as no other president had been during the Cuban missile crisis, and his masterful handling of that crisis was the greatest achievement of his presidency." Dean Acheson, on the other hand, considered that Kennedy had been saved from the consequences of his actions only by "plain dumb luck".

The threat of nuclear extinction could not be ignored in the early 1960s, but some critics have detected a disturbing edge in Jack Kennedy's willingness to summon up this specter at every move, in turn maintaining the atmosphere of permanent crisis which nourished his vision of leadership. The members of ExComm might well have seen themselves as playing in the great drama for which their lives had prepared them, but they were nonetheless playing with the future of the planet. At the end of the course on which they had embarked was the prospect of a world blasted to a cinder.

Jack Kennedy himself later estimated the chances of war at the height of the crisis at something "betweeen one of three and even". This was a pardonable exaggeration. At the time, he had feared that human error rather than Soviet intention might trigger disaster. Significantly, the secret correspondence between the President and Khrushchev which followed the abrasive encounter in Vienna had given each man an insight into the other's character. Kennedy banked on a rational response to the measures he took. By maintaining tight control over the American military response, he narrowed the Soviet options while still leaving a way out for Khrushchev and simultaneously securing what domestic political reality demanded – the removal of the missiles. Later the Soviet leader wrote, "I believe Kennedy was a man who understood the situation correctly and who genuinely did not want war... he showed great flexibility and we avoided disaster."

Each man in his own way was seeking relief from the crushing pressures of the Cold War.

Even being President has its lighter moments. Top left: JFK throwing the first ball in the 1962 baseball season's opening game. Top right: With Dave Powers, a Kennedy aide from 1946 and the President's "Official Greeter" at the White House.

During the crisis, the President had told his old friend David Ormsby Gore, then serving as the British ambassador in Washington, "It really is an intolerable state of affairs when nations can threaten each other with nuclear weapons. This is so totally irrational."

As the two protagonists backed away from the brink, the tensions in the Cold War discernibly relaxed. After the missile crisis, Kennedy and Khrushchev were determined to tackle the nuclear dilemma. The "hot line" was established between Moscow and Washington. Jack Kennedy was particularly concerned with the effect of the radioactive fallout from the atmospheric testing of nuclear devices, which had been resumed by the Soviets in 1961, with the Americans following suit. Jerome Wiesner, Kennedy's special assistant on science and technology, recalled: "The President was deeply concerned about radiocative fallout from testing. He often asked me about this. I remember one day he asked me what happened to the radioactive fallout from testing... and I told him that it was washed out of the clouds by the rain, that it would be brought to earth by rain. And he said, looking out of the window, 'You mean it is in the rain out there?' And I said, 'Yes.' He looked out of the window, looked very sad, and didn't say a word for several minutes."

A degree of arms limitation remained one of Jack Kennedy's consistent goals, and on 7 October 1963 he put his signature to the Nuclear Test Ban treaty, the first disarmament agreement of the nuclear age.

The President signing the Nuclear Test Ban Treaty on 7 October 1963, one of the major personal achievements of his presidency.

Chapter Six

The Last Days of Camelot

The confident Kennedy style caught during a speech in 1962. From diffident beginnings, JFK matured into one of the most formidable orators of his day. Sometimes the sweep of the President's oratory was at odds with his faith in reason, but Theodore White believed that it was Kennedy's gift to animate this cold-seeming quality, so that it "danced".

In the afterglow of public approval of his handling of the Cuban missile crisis, Kennedy's popularity soared at home and abroad. In November, a Gallup poll gave him an approval rating of 74 per cent. From the moment of his victory in November 1961, Jack had been troubled by the narrowness of his margin over Nixon, which had left a question mark hanging over the legitimacy of his presidency. Now, however, he seemed to be clothed in an aura normally associated with royalty. When he took an impromptu swim on a public beach in California, he was followed into the water by an awestruck crowd of wellwishers, including a fully clothed woman who gave every indication of being prepared to swim out after him. Neither the avuncular Ike nor the painfully awkward Nixon could have excited, or would indeed have welcomed, such adulation.

Jack's physical grace and air of apparent accessibility, combined with the dignity of his office, prompted Norman Mailer, in a famous Esquire article, to characterize Jack's accession to the presidency as "Superman Comes to the Supermarket". There was something of the movie star about him; and, as all great movie stars appear to their fans, Jack

Above left: An enthusiatic welcome for the President in New Ross on 28 June 1963 during a four-day trip to Ireland. Dave Powers recalls that during the short visit JFK "grew more Irish by the minute". Above right: Dense crowds line Dublin's O'Connell Street for a glimpse of the President on 27 June. An estimated crowd of half a million Dubliners gave the President a tumultuous welcome. Opposite: JFK's unaffected way with children is in evidence as he extends a hand of encouragement to a small girl in the Kennedys' ancestral home of Dunganstown, from which Patrick Kennedy had set out for America in 1848.

JFK orchestrating one of the regular televised press conferences, staged in the State Department auditorium, which were a prominent feature of his presidency.

seemed so near and yet so far away. None of this happened by chance. Jack was a keen student of his father's genius for the manipulation of the media, and in his turn worked hard on his own image, paying close attention to the smallest details.

A keen golfer, he nevertheless avoided being photographed swinging a club – this would have cast him in the same mold as the elderly Ike, much of whose presidency was passed in a reverie on the links. The rocking chair Jack adopted to ease the pain in his back was transformed from a symbol of physical weakness into an image of folksy relaxation and calm contemplation amid the burdens of office. Vain about his looks, Jack fretted when the regular cortisone injections he still received puffed up his face before his televised press conferences.

The regular press conferences were a striking innovation of his presidency, and he devoted much time and trouble to preparing for them. Relaxed and confident, he dealt with the press in masterful fashion while seldom saying anything of great substance. As James Reston recalled, he overwhelmed his deferential inquisitors with "decimal points" or disarmed them "with a smile and a wisecrack". These performances were as important as FDR's "fireside chats" in bringing the President into the homes of the American people to deliver messages of reassurance and hope and, in the exhortatory fashion to which his rhetoric was attuned, to urge the nation to further effort and sacrifice.

In all of this the press was a willing accomplice. Like the ambassador, the President was an assiduous cultivator of influential journalists and their proprietors. It was his idea to invite America's leading publishers to lunch in the White House on a state-by-state basis. And such were the heady attractions of the proximity to power and assimilation into the charmed circle of the Kennedys that many journalists surrendered their objectivity when dealing with Jack and his family. A revealing presidential note, handwritten just before the Bay of Pigs fiasco, asked, "Is there a plan to brainwash the press within twelve hours or so?" and then went on to list a number of distinguished commentators. The note was redundant, as many journalists had already been brainwashed by Kennedy mystique and manipulation into becoming unofficial spokesmen for the administration.

Every monarch must have his consort and, in Jacqueline Bouvier, Jack Kennedy found a "fairytale princess" whose beauty and impeccable taste animated the "Camelot" legend which sprang up around Jack's presidency after his death. The reality of their marriage was rather different to the legend. It had come close to ending in divorce in 1956, shortly after Jack's unsuccessful bid for the vice-presidential nomination. Jack took himself off to a yacht in the Mediterranean, where he consoled himself with a blonde bimbo who referred to herself in the third person as "Pooh". Jackie remained at home to deliver a stillborn child. It took three days for Jack's

An informal portrait of the President and first lady, taken in Evelyn Lincoln's office, adjoining the Oval Office, after Jackie had been out riding. Ted Sorensen found the first lady "sensitive but strong-willed ... By maintaining her own unique identity and provocative personality, she never bored or wearied the President ".

friend Senator George Smathers to persuade him to return to his wife, who was critically ill after losing their child.

The marriage was patched up – divorce would have spelled the end of Jack's political career – and thereafter Jackie took a form of revenge on her philandering husband with a mania for the endless redecoration of their homes, which made them virtually uninhabitable for much of the time and which drove the penny-pinching Jack to distraction.

The refurbishment of the White House presented Jackie with her greatest challenge, and much of the cultural dazzle of Jack's presidency derived from his wife's taste and inclinations rather than his own. He had pledged himself to the pursuit of excellence in all aspects of national life, and in the White House played debonair host to André Malraux, Igor Stravinsky and, most famously, to the cellist Pablo Casals, who had last played there in 1904 for Teddy Roosevelt. Left to his

*JFK congratulates Pablo Casals after his
concert in the White House on 13 November
1961.*

During JFK's presidency Jackie became a
public figure in her own right. Her solo trip to
India and Pakistan in 1962 was a public
relations triumph. Here she enjoys a joke with
Indira Gandhi and India's Prime Minister
Jawaharlal Nehru. The stork-like figure of
J.K. Galbraith, US ambassador to India,
looms on the right.

own devices, however, Jack preferred listening to the country and western music piped into the White House swimming pool, and reading Ian Fleming's James Bond thrillers, whose worldwide popularity dates from press reports that they were among the President's favorite books.

The poets and Nobel prize winners who flocked to the White House enabled Jack Kennedy to cast himself in the role of philosopher-statesman, a patrician patron of the arts along the lines of the largely imaginary British aristocracy he had admired since 1939. No matter that he had no idea who Casals was until Jackie told him; as the ambassador had impressed upon him in his adolescence, the important thing is not what you are but what people think you are. In this skillfully engineered contrast between youthful Kennedy urbanity and Eisenhower's provincialism the artists, musicians and writers themselves were as willing participants as Washington's house-trained journalists.

Glittering as were these strenuous celebrations of the New Frontier's cultural correctness, Jack probably preferred the two birthday celebrations brashly choreographed for him by Broadway luminary Richard Adler, who attested that "This was the President's party, not one of those culture-vulture programs".

At the first, held in Madison Square Garden, Jack was serenaded by Marilyn Monroe who sang *Happy Birthday, dear Mr President,* her ripe body sheathed revealingly in an outfit she described as "skin and beads". Jackie did not attend. Arthur Schlesinger remembered Bobby Kennedy "dodging around Marilyn like a moth round a flame". Jack had first enjoyed the movie star's favors in the 1950s but during his presidency both men were among her lovers. Photographs taken of Marilyn on the night of Jack's forty-fifth birthday party, on 19 May 1962, poignantly expose her ravaged beauty and fragility. None survive showing her with the President. Distressed, abandoned and awash with drugs, Marilyn died, apparently by her own hand, on 4 August 1962.

Jack's compulsive womanizing did not cease when he entered the White House. If anything the office seemed to accelerate his sexual drive. While Pablo Casals went in the front door, numerous less distinguished guests were smuggled in and out of the back. Jack's falls from grace have been well documented, from the casual fling he enjoyed at journalist Joe Alsop's house on the night of his inauguration to affairs with actress Angie Dickinson, journalist Ben Bradlee's sister-in-law Mary Pinchot Meyer, with whom he smoked marijuana in the White House, and the two freshfaced young White House secretaries nicknamed "Fiddle" and "Faddle".

There was considerable risk attached to these activities, but it was a risk Jack Kennedy actively courted, even if, as happened at least once, his sexual urge separated him from the officer bearing the briefcase which contained the nuclear codes. Potentially the most

The man in the spotlight. The President enjoying his 45th birthday party, held at Madison Square Garden on 19 May 1962, choreographed in Broadway style by Richard Adler. It was on this memorable occasion that he was serenaded by Marilyn Monroe, poured into a skin-tight dress and singing "Happy Birthday, dear Mr President". In his speech JFK responded by telling the audience, "I can now retire from politics after having had, ah, 'Happy Birthday' sung to me in such a sweet and wholesome way." Jackie did not attend the birthday party, preferring instead to take part in a Virginia horse show.

The President with Jimmy Durante at a private party after the official celebrations for his 45th birthday at Madison Square Garden. Standing behind Durante is Vaughn Meader, the comedian whose impressions of JFK brought him a brief celebrity. JFK and Marilyn Monroe were the principal attractions at the party but no photographs survive of Marilyn with the President.

compromising of Kennedy's extra-marital relationships was that with Judith Campbell (later Judith Campbell-Exner) to whom he was introduced by Frank Sinatra in March 1960. Campbell, a dark beauty reminiscent of Elizabeth Taylor, was also the mistress of Sam Giancana, and on a number of occasions carried packages and communications between Kennedy and the mobster. At the time Giancana was simultaneously being harried by the FBI and was assisting the CIA in their risible attempts to assassinate Castro. Campbell visited Jack regularly in the White House when Jackie was away at Glen Ora, the family's retreat in Virginia. At one point, in a fit of almost suicidal bravado, Jack tried to persuade Campbell to accompany him on Air Force One.

The affair, and Kennedy's friendship with Frank Sinatra, were brought to an end after Jack entertained J. Edgar Hoover to lunch on 22 March 1962. It can scarcely have been an agreeable meal. Hoover was the one Washington bureaucrat immune from the guerrilla raids of the New Frontiersmen. Knowledge is power, and Hoover had accumulated too much about the Kennedys for them to contemplate moving against him. Revelations about Jack's relationship with Campbell and hers with Giancana would have dealt a deadly blow, not only to Attorney-General Bobby Kennedy's continuing war against organized crime but also to the office of the presidency.

Jack's recklessness was not confined to his sexual adventures. In the summer of 1961 he became increasingly reliant on the amphetamines administered for the relief of his back pain by Dr Max Jacobson – a quack later struck off – to whom he had been introduced in 1960. Jacobson accompanied Kennedy to the Vienna summit and also treated the President during the Cuban missile crisis. At one point, Kennedy was keen to install Jacobson, whose nickname among his showbusiness friends was "Dr Feelgood", in the White House. When confronted by an agitated Bobby with hard evidence about the nature of Jacobson's quack remedies, Jack retorted, "I don't care if it's horse piss. It works." A lifetime of pain had perhaps clouded his judgment on Jacobson's shots and the effect they might have on his decision-making ability.

Jack Kennedy's determination to demonstrate American strength and resolve to Moscow and Peking was the overriding concern in his strategy for a first term. Moreover, he was faced with a largely hostile Congress and, as a result, the domestic achievement of the Kennedy administration remained modest. The majority of the reforms of the New Frontier – including medical care for the elderly, urban renewal, federal aid for education and urban mass transportation, youth employment and migrant assistance measures – were not enacted until after his death. However, there was one domestic issue which assumed such urgency during his "One Thousand Days" that it threatened to

unbalance his foreign policy initiatives. Civil rights, around which Kennedy had maneuvered so adroitly since the mid-1950s, were to provide a stern test of the administration's ability to fulfil the expectations which had been raised by his rhetoric.

While campaigning for the presidency, Kennedy sought advice from Harris Wofford on civil rights, telling him that "I'm way behind on this, because I've hardly known any blacks in my life. It isn't an issue I've thought about a lot, and I've got to catch up fast." Just how fast was soon evident.

Jack Kennedy had an intellectual understanding of the entrenched racism in American society and a natural distaste for the bigoted excesses of the South, but there was little or no moral fervor in his approach to civil rights, which was circumscribed by his easy relations with Southern politicians and the knowledge that he had been helped over the top in November 1960 by 81 Southern electoral votes. He saw the eradication of racism as a problem to be managed rather than a cause to be championed.

This set Kennedy at odds not only with the Democratic Party's election pledges on civil rights but also with the hopes of reform he had encouraged, notably with his telephone call to Coretta King. Significantly, though, of the twenty-nine "task forces" set up in the early weeks of the administration, there was none for civil rights. No new civil rights legislation was introduced. Reluctant to become bogged down in a dogfight with Congress, Kennedy told black leaders that civil rights legislation would "bottleneck" other measures, including those which he considered important to the black cause. Nor did Kennedy fulfil his campaign pledge to end discrimination in federally funded housing projects with an executive order he had described as "one stroke of the pen". His reluctance to meet this commitment prompted a steady stream of reproachful pens posted to the White House. The President was nonetheless alive to the problem and attempted to demonstrate his good intentions with a program of executive action. During his inaugural parade he had noticed that there were no black cadets in the contingent from the Coast Guard Academy. Within hours he gave instructions for the admission of blacks to the Academy.

In its first two months the administration appointed forty blacks to significant posts, including Robert Weaver, president of the National Association for the Advancement of Colored People (NAACP), who became administrator of the Housing and Home Finance Agency. Five blacks were appointed to federal judgeships, including the first two in the continental United States. Thurgood Marshall, the foremost lawyer in the NAACP, was appointed to the Second Circuit of Appeals in New York. The Civil Rights section of the Justice Department pressed hard to enforce court orders and existing legislation, particularly in the field of voting rights. In the South, however, its efforts were deliberately blocked by a number of federal judges appointed by Kennedy as part of the political horsetrading with the South, among whom was William Harold Cox, who had compared blacks with chimpanzees and referred to them as "niggers" in court. Pragmatism was also at work in the President's Committee on Equal Employment Opportunity, created by executive order in March 1961 and a largely ineffectual body, chaired by Lyndon Johnson, which aimed to encourage business to reduce discrimination.

The administration's gradualist approach was overtaken by events on the streets of the South which began in the summer of 1961 when two buses of whites and blacks – the Freedom Riders – launched a campaign to challenge racism and segregation at lunch counters and in rest rooms. This non-violent assault on the citadels of white oppression triggered a brutal backlash which threatened to embarrass Kennedy as he prepared to meet Khrushchev at Vienna. Angrily, he told Harris Wofford, who was now working at the Justice Department, to "get your people off those buses".

The violence grew worse. In Montgomery, Alabama, the President's personal representative, a tough cowboy-booted Tennesseean named John Seigenthaler, was beaten unconscious as he attempted to rescue a young black woman from a racist attack. For half an hour he lay on the sidewalk, unattended, while FBI agents stood around and watched. When Martin Luther King

The President addressing the United Nations on 25 September 1961, a week after the death of UN Secretary General Dag Hammarskjold in an air crash in Africa. It was in this speech that JFK challenged the Soviet Union to a "peace race".

arrived in Montgomery to hold a church service, he had to be protected from a howling mob by 50 of the 500 US marshals sent to the city by the Attorney General to maintain order.

The Kennedy brothers' hopes that the passions aroused by the civil rights campaign would be calmed by a combination of conciliation, modest voting rights measures, black economic improvement and backstairs arm-twisting were dashed in 1962. In September a twenty-nine-year-old black, James Meredith, attempted to enrol in the University of Mississippi in Oxford. The ensuing riots were only brought under control by the belated arrival of 23,000 troops, all of them white.

Meredith was enrolled but Martin Luther King was left with the sour feeling that he was merely "a pawn in the white man's game" as the Kennedy brothers maneuvered behind the scenes with Southern politicians to limit the political damage. Moreover, the reform process seemed painfully slow. It was only in November 1962 that Jack Kennedy finally announced a watered-down housing order prohibiting discrimination in federally assisted housing. The measure was sandwiched between statements on the withdrawal of Soviet bombers from Cuba and the Sino-Indian border conflict.

The President continued to resist demands for civil rights legislation. His sensitivity on the issue was revealed when, at a White House reception for civil rights activists to commemorate the Emancipation proclamation, attended by many blacks, the presence of Sammy Davis Jr and his Swedish wife Mai Britt led to a ban on press photographers. He also publicly rejected the findings of an independent liberal body, the Civil Rights Commission, on the race terror in Mississippi.

The administration was swimming against a powerful tide which finally overwhelmed it in the spring of 1963 when Martin Luther King chose Birmingham, Alabama, as the target for a campaign to integrate department store lunch counters. The city's Police Commissioner, Eugene "Bull" Connors, and his men obliged the waiting cameras by unleashing savage dogs and turning high-pressure fire hoses on the largely non-violent demonstrators. A nation of television viewers was appalled by the spectacle of naked hatred, while in cities across America blacks took matters into their own hands in a wave of civil disturbances. Black Muslim leader Malcolm X fanned his own form of racial hatred, and moderate civil rights leaders assumed a more militant tone. In Chicago Martin Luther King declared, "We can't wait any longer. Now is the time." In Tuscaloosa on 11 June 1963 the segregationist governor of Alabama, George Wallace, stood in the doorway of the University of Alabama in a well-publicized protest against the admission of two black students.

At 8pm on the same day Kennedy addressed the nation on television. The first

Victims of police brutality in Birmingham, Alabama. Civil rights presented the Kennedy administration with its most severe domestic crisis and prompted JFK to wrap his frustration at the endemic racism in American society in the scathing comment that, "The United States Government is sitting down at Geneva with the Soviet Union. I can't understand why the city council of Albany, Georgia, cannot do the same for American citizens."

draft of his speech was completed only three minutes before he went on air and he extemporized the conclusion from his notes. He told the American people: "One hundred years of delay have passed since President Lincoln freed the slaves, yet their heirs, their grandsons, are not fully free. They are not yet freed from their bonds of injustice. They are not yet freed from social and economic repression. And this nation, for all its hopes and boasts, will not be fully free until all its citizens are free."

Having seized the high moral ground, albeit somewhat belatedly, Kennedy announced that the crisis could not be "quieted by token measures or talk". He intended to submit to Congress legislation which ensured equal access to public accommodation and which strengthened federal voting, employment and education guarantees.

The pledge did not halt the violence. On the night of Kennedy's speech Medgar Evers, a representative of the NAACP, was murdered outside his home in Jackson, Mississippi. Riots followed his funeral. In Washington Bobby Kennedy, brandishing a bullhorn, personally confronted 3,000 black protesters marching on the Justice Department.

An altogether bigger march on Washington was now being prepared to rally support for civil rights legislation. Fearing a bloodbath, the Kennedy brothers attempted to have the march called off. When this failed they minimized the risk of riot by supervising every

detail. Apprehensive that an overwhelmingly black march on Capitol Hill would hinder the passage of the Civil Rights Bill, they drafted in thousands of whites from labor and church organizations to swell the ranks of the marchers. The fiery speeches which some activists planned to deliver were edited by the Assistant Attorney General, Burke Marshall.

The march, involving some 250,000 people, went ahead on 28 August. Martin Luther King told them "I have a dream" while another student of rhetoric, Jack Kennedy, watched the speech on television. King was also being watched closely by the FBI. Convinced that he was a tool of the Communists, J. Edgar Hoover had used his hold over the Kennedys to get Bobby to agree to wiretaps being placed on King. Meanwhile, on Capitol Hill, Jack was struggling to win bipartisan support for the Civil Rights Bill. He told a black leader, "This issue could cost me the election, but we're not turning back." The Bill was not enacted until after his death.

On 28 August, while the civil rights marchers converged on the Lincoln Memorial, Jack Kennedy had chaired a meeting on the mounting crisis in Vietnam. The tragedy of Vietnam has cast a long retrospective shadow over Kennedy's administration, but when he took office the problems of that country were not among the New Frontiersmen's top priorities. When Bobby was asked about Vietnam, he had replied brusquely, "Vietnam? We have thirty Vietnams a day."

At the beginning of 1961 the focus of

The civil rights march on Washington, August 1963. In his television address from the White House on 11 June the President had told the nation: "We preach freedom around the world, and we mean it. And we cherish our freedom here at home. But are we to say to the world, and, much more importantly, to each other, that this is a land of the free except for the Negroes ..."

attention in Southeast Asia was neighboring Laos, where since 1953 a war had been fought between the Communist Pathet Lao insurgents, whose principal backers were the North Vietnamese, and the Royal Laotian Army, which was bankrolled by the United States. On the day before he assumed the presidency, Kennedy was briefed by Eisenhower, who placed great emphasis on the situation in Laos, warning that if the country fell to the Communists it would force the United States to write off Southeast Asia.

In reality things were rather more complicated. Chastened by his experience in the Bay of Pigs, Kennedy resisted pressure from the Joint Chiefs of Staff to defeat the Communists with a large-scale military commitment. Riven by factions, Laos was effectively a non-country incapable of being sustained by an American-backed strongman or held together by a neutralist government which, it was feared, would inevitably fall into the orbit of the Communists. Nevertheless, it was under the cloak of neutrality that an attempt was made to salvage something from the wreckage. The Geneva Accords, signed in July 1962 with the blessing of the United States and the Soviet Union, established a government under a prominent neutralist, Prince Souvanna Phouma. All non-Laotian forces were required to withdraw and paramilitary assistance was to cease.

Subsequently the war was continued by covert means. The North Vietnamese, who did not consider themselves answerable to the Soviet Union, maintained a strong military presence in Laos, training and equipping the Pathet Lao and funneling their Viet Cong irregulars into Vietnam along the Ho Chi Minh Trail, which passed through the jungles of southeastern Laos. The American response was a counterinsurgency program in which nearly 40,000 Laotian tribesmen and Thai "volunteers" were recruited by the CIA, which also used its airline, Air America, in a bombing campaign against the Pathet Lao. The Soviet Union turned a blind eye to the CIA's secret war, which grew into a huge paramilitary effort costing millions of dollars a year.

While the Bay of Pigs fiasco had discouraged Kennedy from an overt military intervention in Laos, the hectoring to which he had been subjected by Khrushchev at Vienna seems to have hardened his determination to make a stand in Vietnam. The commentator James Reston recalled that at the conclusion of the summit Kennedy had told him that "he had tried to convince Khrushchev of US determination but had failed. It was now essential to demonstrate our firmness, and the place to do it, he remarked to my astonishment, was Vietnam! I don't think I swallowed his hat, but I was speechless. If he had said he was going to run the Communist blockade into Berlin, I might have understood, but the reference to Vietnam baffled me."

Reston's bafflement apart, there were few American politicians better qualified than Jack Kennedy to tackle the problems posed by Vietnam. Since his 1951 visit to Southeast Asia

The President holds a press conference on the crisis in Laos in March 1961. But it was the shadow of North Vietnam which later hung over assessments of his presidency.

he had immersed himself in the problems of the region. He was a founder-member of the Friends of Vietnam and was an acquaintance of its premier, the Catholic Ngo Dinh Diem. In a series of speeches in the 1950s he had expressed his doubts about the United States' ability to defeat the Communist threat with an open-ended military commitment. His skepticism was confirmed when he became president. Waiting for him was an extremely gloomy report about Vietnam, prepared for the Eisenhower administration by General Edward Lansdale, the Pentagon's leading expert in guerrilla warfare.

Lansdale had returned from Vietnam convinced that the corrupt, inefficient Diem government was unprepared psychologically, militarily and in every other respect to fight the Communist Viet Cong guerrillas, whose political arm, the National Liberation Front (NLF), was exerting an increasingly tight grip over the countryside. The South Vietnamese army was as corrupt as the regime it served; officered by incompetent political appointees and trained by its American advisers to rely on firepower, it had neither the flexibility nor the will to counter its guerrilla enemy. At the same time Diem resisted the implementation of a Counterinsurgency Plan originated by the Eisenhower administration, and urged on him by Kennedy, which tied increased military aid to political reforms.

In May 1961 Vice-President Lyndon Johnson was sent to Vietnam on a fact-finding mission. Initially reluctant to go – his

departure was speeded by adding members of the Kennedy family to his party as "hostages" – Johnson returned full of enthusiasm for Diem, extravagantly describing him as the Winston Churchill of Southeast Asia. Nailing his colors to the mast, Johnson declared, "The basic decision in Southeast Asia is here: we must decide whether to help these countries to the best of our ability or throw in the towel in the area and pull back our defenses to San Francisco ..."

While Johnson hobnobbed with the Churchillian leader of South Vietnam, Kennedy secretly approved the despatch of 400 Special Forces troops and 100 US advisers to Vietnam, in violation of the Geneva agreement of 1954. They were to train South Vietnamese personnel to fight a clandestine war against the North. US civilians were cleared to fly as air crew on "appropriate" missions in this campaign.

At the same time Kennedy was receiving military advice that the guerrilla strength in South Vietnam had risen to 17,000. He remained indecisive throughout the summer of 1961, preoccupied with the Vienna summit and the Berlin crisis, while major divisions opened up in the administration over policy on Vietnam. The Joint Chiefs of Staff considered that "40,000 US troops will be needed to clear up the Viet Cong threat". Secretary of State Rusk, then a skeptic, considered it unwise to commit the United States to backing Diem, whom he considered "a losing horse".

Another mission was sent to Saigon

The President strides out with Vice-President Lyndon Johnson keeping station at his shoulder, like a staff officer with his commanding general. During his presidency JFK had some difficulty in finding an outlet for LBJ's restless energies.

headed by Walt Rostow and General Maxwell Taylor, a former Chief of Staff of the US Army and an "intellectual" soldier much admired by Jack Kennedy, who had brought him in from retirement to conduct the inquest on the Bay of Pigs operation. They arrived in Saigon on the day Diem declared a state of emergency and requested increased military aid.

Taylor reported that a force of 8,000 troops should be sent to Vietnam to provide technical and combat assistance in return for political reforms undertaken by Diem. He considered that "as an area for operations of US troops, South Vietnam is not an excessively difficult or unpleasant place to operate".

Alarmed by the implications of Taylor's report, George Ball confronted the President at the beginning of November, warning him that "within five years you will have 300,000 men in the paddies and jungles and never find them again ... Vietnam is the worst possible terrain from the physical and political point of view". To which Kennedy replied, "I always thought you were one of the brightest guys in town, but you're just crazier than hell."

Kennedy did not follow Taylor's recommendation, but did send 300 helicopter pilots to South Vietnam. In February 1962 a Military Assistance Command Vietnam (MACV) was established under General Paul D. Harkins. Driven by Robert McNamara's insatiable appetite for figures with which to "quantify" progress in Vietnam – he was forever brandishing graphs which "proved" that victory was in sight – MACV relied on

data fabricated by the South Vietnamese, who were eager to please their paymasters. As a result MACV's optimism bordered on the pathological. By the end of 1962 there were 12,000 US military advisers in Vietnam.

Kennedy had become the prisoner of his own doctrine of "flexible response". Having emerged triumphant from the Cuban missile crisis, he was confident that the chances of nuclear war had been significantly reduced and that a *modus vivendi* could be reached with Moscow and Peking after an unequivocal demonstration of American resolve to resist "national wars of liberation".

Central to this strategy was a flexible response to Communist expansion in the Third World – the diversification of forces to permit graduated responses to differing military situations in which Special Forces, expanded troop-lift capability and counterinsurgency tactics would all play a part. In this waging of "limited war", counterinsurgency held a particular fascination for Jack Kennedy, who acknowledged the charismatic qualities of men like Che Guevara and devoured the military writings of Mao-Tse Tung in an attempt to get to know his enemy. In October 1961 he insisted that the US Special Forces readopt the famous green beret, and throughout his presidency demonstrated an almost schoolboyish enthusiasm for the minutiae of jungle warfare. Any New Frontiersman who wanted to get on had to scramble aboard the counterinsurgency bandwagon, and Washington positively throbbed with think tanks and seminars

The President watches astronaut John Glenn on the first American orbital flight, 20 February 1962. At his shoulder are Lyndon Johnson and Senator Hubert Humphrey. On 12 September 1962 JFK told an audience of 35,000 people at Rice University, Houston, Texas: "We choose to go the moon. We choose to go to the moon in this decade, and do the other things, not because they are easy but because they are hard; because that goal will serve to organize and measure the best of our energies and skills ... What was once the farthest outpost on the old frontier of the West will be the farthest outpost on the new frontier of science and space." The President's promise to go to the moon was fulfilled in 1969.

analyzing the philosophy and tactics of the subject. General Taylor was appointed to head an interagency body, Special Group, Counterinsurgency, and a White House task force was formed to consider its application to Vietnam.

There was an inherent danger attached to this approach, for it encouraged the very kind of military adventurism which could draw the United States into a conflict from which it could not easily disengage. Massive retaliation imposed its own terrible restraint, but a conviction that a limited war could be fought and won implied that any failure to meet a Communist advance, whether small or large, would be interpreted as a slackening of American will. And in a world in which the Kennedy administration saw itself confronting one crisis after another, this could not be allowed. Arguing over Vietnam with John Kenneth Galbraith, then US ambassador to India, Kennedy said, "There are limits to the number of defeats I can defend in one twelve-month period. I've had the Bay of Pigs and pulling out of Laos, and I can't accept a third:"

With 12,000 advisers in South Vietnam the US Army was now playing an operational role, following its own decisions and chain of command and exacerbating the tensions between those who advocated a military solution and those who still saw the situation in South Vietnam in political terms. The Diem regime, aptly described as a combination of the Borgias and the Bourbons, soon rendered these arguments academic. Incapable of initiating any meaningful reforms, it now increased its unpopularity with a campaign of harassment against the Buddhist religion, to which 70 per cent of the South Vietnamese population adhered. When a number of Buddhist monks burned themselves to death in protest, Diem's sister-in-law, Madame Nhu, described the incidents as "barbecues".

In August 1963 the US ambassador in Saigon, Frederick "Fritz" Nolting, a staunch supporter of Diem, was replaced by Kennedy's old adversary Henry Cabot Lodge, whose thankless task was to encourage behavior from the Diem regime which was more acceptable to the American public. Immediately on his arrival he was approached by a group of South Vietnamese generals sounding out the possibility of US support for a military coup. When Lodge cabled Washington for instructions he received a reply which was, to say the least, ambivalent. Roger Hilsman, then Assistant Secretary of State for Far Eastern Affairs, has elaborated on the reply that was sent to Lodge: "The overall gist of the cable was to say that we would prefer a government continuing under Diem, but if they felt that they had no choice, then we would examine the government that they established on its own merits. Now, of course, there is no question that this, with all its hedges, did encourage them."

The administration was cutting Diem adrift, but it was slow-motion drama compounded by the South Vietnamese

The right stuff. The President, accompanied by Lieutenant-Colonel John Glenn, examines the Friendship 7 capsule which took Glenn on the first American orbital flight on 20 February 1962.

generals' reluctance to strike and the guarded language the administration was careful to use in its private communications and public statements. When Lodge pressed Kennedy to prod the dithering South Vietnamese generals into action, the President replied, "We will do all that we can to help you conclude this operation successfully," adding, "I must reserve a contingent right to change course and revise previous instructions." On 2 September,

in a TV interview with Walter Cronkite, Kennedy suggested that the Diem regime "had gotten out of touch with the people". When asked if there was still time to save the political situation in Vietnam, he replied that there was "with changes in policy and, perhaps, with personnel".

Ten days later Kennedy emphasized that the United States was not in Vietnam "to see a war lost" and hinted that aid to South Vietnam would be cut off and the advisers withdrawn if Diem did not mend his ways. Diem was immune to such threats, and on 1 November, the generals – having finally plucked up their courage – overthrew and murdered him. When he received the news, Jack Kennedy was visibly moved. Nevertheless, CIA director William Colby later commented, "This was the Vietnamese generals' coup, yes, but I think the fundamentals of it were decided in our White House". As many had predicted, Diem's downfall produced only greater political chaos in South Vietnam and with it the "Americanization" of the war under Kennedy's successor, Lyndon Johnson.

Three weeks after Diem's death Jack Kennedy was assassinated. His record on Vietnam remains cloudy. Remembering the ignominious defeat that had overtaken the French, he never lost sight of the dangers of a deep American involvement. Nevertheless, he had significantly increased that involvement, and at the time of his death there were 17,000 US troops in Vietnam. With some reluctance he had sanctioned the limited use of napalm and defoliants and the introduction of "free fire zones". Privately he had expressed misgivings about the American commitment. Early in 1963 he had confided in Mike Mansfield, the Democratic Majority Leader in the Senate and a Catholic who had visited Vietnam and was critical of US involvement. Mansfield remembered: "He called me down and said he had changed his mind and that he wanted to begin to withdraw from Vietnam, beginning the first of the following year, that would be in January 1964. He was very unhappy about the situation which he had developed there and he felt that even then with 16,000 troops we were in far too deep." Before he was assassinated, Kennedy ordered the withdrawal of 1,000 troops from South Vietnam.

Against this and other recollections may be placed the accounts of those to whom Kennedy spoke out of the other side of his mouth, for example Dean Rusk, who later asserted, "I had hundreds of talks with President Kennedy about Vietnam and on no single occasion did he ever express to me any idea on that line". Bobby Kennedy, to whom Jack was closest, later said, "The President felt he had a strong, overwhelming reason for being in Vietnam and that we should win the war". As he had initially and mistakenly calculated over civil rights, Jack Kennedy was maneuvering to postpone hard decisions on Vietnam until after the 1964 election. Precipitate withdrawal before then would only hand a powerful weapon to the American Right. Faced with fundamentally conflicting assessments of the war, ranging from McNamara's optimistic prediction that victory would be secured by the end of 1965 to warnings that already "the Indians were coming through the windows", the President remained confident that he could play for time while continuing to emphasize publicly that it was for the South Vietnamese to win their own war, with American materiel aid. A vain hope.

The President watches a fly-past at Fort Bragg in December 1961 on a day when the entire 82nd Airborne Division of 16,000 men was drawn up for him to review.

By degrees he had exposed himself to a crisis which was not amenable to any simple solution.

Having failed to get to grips with the political problem in Vietnam, the Kennedy administration's military build-up, albeit of non-combat troops, gave the Pentagon a decisive operational lever with which to influence policy. In 1951 as a young congressman Jack Kennedy had pumped journalists for the real story of what was happening in Vietnam. As president, he had railed against equally critical reports filed by American journalists in Saigon, accusing them of being unpatriotic and in individual cases attempting to get them recalled. The advisers and policy which passed from Jack Kennedy to Lyndon Johnson plunged the United States deeper into the mire. Had he lived, he would have exercised a more flexible and considered military or diplomatic policy than his successor, but this is to reckon without the absolute determination of the North Vietnamese to secure their objectives come what may. The Americans were just the latest in the long line of powerful interlopers seen off by the Vietnamese in their long history. When one is caught in a quagmire, it matters little whether one slid in stylishly or not.

On 13 November 1963 the President called together his top political strategists to begin planning the 1964 campaign. As they gathered in the Cabinet Room late that afternoon, thoughts turned back to the meeting at Hyannis Port on Thanksgiving Day 1959 at which the strategy for the presidential campaign had been decided.

There was every reason for optimism. At home the economy was booming, with gross national product running at $100 billion over the 1960 figure. The civil rights crisis had been negotiated without damaging the administration, and the introduction of the Civil Rights Bill had enabled Kennedy to narrow the troubling gap between his highflown rhetoric and political reality. The signing of the limited test ban treaty with the Soviet Union – which Kennedy had skillfully steered through initial opposition from the military and some members of his own administration – signaled a gradual unfreezing of the Cold War. His sensitive political antennae detected not only cracks in the monstrous edifice of the Cold War but also a shift in public opinion away from confrontation. By degrees he was moving toward accommodation with the Soviet Union.

In a speech delivered at American University on 10 June he had spoken of "peace as the necessary, rational end of rational man," and in a particularly moving passage told the audience, "... in the final analysis, our most basic common link is that we all inhabit this small planet. We all breathe the same air. We all cherish our children's future. And we are all mortal."

In the same speech Kennedy had said, "we can seek a relaxation of tensions without relaxing our guard". During his presidency the United States had increased its military strength in a surge of spending which some critics have claimed defied all rational standards of productivity and cost/quality control achieved since 1942. As a result, this "rational" president, who had agonized so deeply over the intolerable pressures of the Cold War and the baleful effects of fall-out, had achieved the most rapid strategic military build-up in the peacetime history of his country. He doubled the number of Polaris submarines, increased Minuteman ICBM purchases by 75 per cent, the number of tactical nuclear weapons deployed in Europe by 60 per cent and the total number of weapons in the US nuclear arsenal by 100 per cent. At the end of November he planned to visit Cape Canaveral to inspect the new Saturn I rocket, the most powerful ever built, which was scheduled to make its first flight in December. The fictitious "missile gap" which had haunted Americans at the end of the 1950s had now been laid to rest and the United States could begin to overhaul the Soviets in the manned spacecraft race. In turn, the Soviets were forced to respond, placing strains on their chaotic command economy which, in the long term, could not be sustained. Here, perhaps, lies one of the compelling reasons for the break-up of the Soviet Union and the ending of the Cold War which had fueled the energies of the Kennedy administration. During his presidency, Jack Kennedy had sensed signs of the unfreezing of

JFK shares a joke with Barry Goldwater at a ceremony in the White House Rose Garden honoring retiring USAF General Emmett "Rosie" O'Donnell. By the autumn of 1963 it was clear that Goldwater would be the Republican Presidential challenger in 1964.

Left: Joshing with Press Secretary Pierre Salinger during the 1962 America's Cup races. Salinger, who was not a man of the great outdoors, was a trifle overdressed for the occasion. The President's response was to rub it in by loosening his tie and posing for photographer Cecil Stoughton. Opposite: JFK on board the USS Andrew Jackson watching a test launch of the Polaris missile. The photograph was taken six days before his assassination.

relations between East and West, but on both sides these fissures were still hidden under the permafrost of Cold War posturing. Jack, too, had been a Cold War warrior, and he was still moving toward the psychological adjustment necessary for a breakthrough. Therefore, there is some irony in the fact that his greatest contribution to the unraveling of the Soviet empire lay in massive military expenditure.

Fitter than he had been for years, increasingly secure in his popularity and in his marriage which was now entering a phase of greater stability and understanding, and no longer dogged by the narrowness of the victory he had achieved over Nixon, Kennedy looked forward to trouncing the likely Republican candidate, the right-wing Barry Goldwater, in

the 1964 election, and the implementation of his deferred program of domestic reform by a more compliant Congress. Meanwhile there was a little local political difficulty to smooth over in Texas, where a squabble between two of the state's leading Democrats, Governor John Connally and Senator Ralph Yarborough, threatened to disrupt preparations for the presidential campaign.

In Fort Worth, Texas, on the morning of 22 November, Jack Kennedy seemed at his most relaxed. As a light rain fell he gave a short, extemporized speech in the parking lot of his hotel, telling the crowd, "Mrs Kennedy is organizing herself. It takes longer. But, of course, she looks far better than we do when she does it."

"Is there a rabbit under my desk?" The President and his son John indulge in a regular ritual of hide and seek which took place before the little boy went to bed. JFK's unforced affection for children was one of his most endearing personal traits, and it shines through in all the photographs in which he appears with his own and other people's offspring. In August 1963, waiting in the hospital where the life of his baby son Patrick was slipping away, he still found time to comfort a small child who had been badly burned. Opposite: JFK with his daughter Caroline.

Above: The President meets a small fan hoisted over the heads of the crowd in Billings, Montana, during a tour of conservation areas in 1963. It was on this tour that he began to sound out public opinion on his growing desire for détente with the Soviet Union. Right: Trick or treat. The President gets a Halloween surprise from Caroline in a witch's costume, a recalcitrant black cat and John as Peter-Panda. Opposite: One of JFK's favorite photographs – playtime in the Oval Office with Caroline and John.

After another more formal speech in the hotel, where he declined to don a stetson, just as he had gone bareheaded in Boston in 1946, the President's party made the short flight to Dallas in Air Force One, its interior resplendently redecorated by Raymond Loewy, the man who designed the Coca-Cola dispenser. Air Force One touched down at Love Field at 11.39am, local time, and sixteen minutes later the President's motorcade was bound for Dallas.

It was a hot, clear day and the bullet-proof glass bubble was not fitted to Jack Kennedy's Lincoln. Into Dallas he swept through cheering crowds. Noticing a banner which read "Mr President, Please Stop and Shake our Hands", he ordered his limousine to stop and leaned out to shake the hands of a group of children. The motorcade drove on through Dallas, down Main Street, past Police Headquaters, along Field Street and into Dealey Plaza, where Jack Kennedy's assassins waited for him.

Tens of millions of words have been spilled on the assassination of Jack Kennedy and there is no sign that the flow is about to cease. Few people now believe the Warren Commission's conclusion that Lee Harvey Oswald was a lone assassin. If, as the Congressional Assasinations Committee concluded in 1979, there was a conspiracy to kill the president, the question remains as to who was behind it. Far-fetched theories have been advanced which implicate Lyndon Johnson and the entire "military-industrial complex", about whose unwarranted influence

Eisenhower had warned in his farewell address in January 1961 and which, conspiracy theorists believe, was alarmed at the prospect of Kennedy ending the American commitment to Vietnam. Kennedy's ruminations, it would appear, had caused them to fear for their future profits. However, the massive conventional and nuclear build-up during the Kennedy years had served the interests of the "military-industrial complex"; and Jack's readiness to contemplate military responses to the most serious foreign policy crises of his presidency demonstrate that he was, if anything, a functional representative of these forces rather than an enemy to be removed.

The evidence now available points toward the murky convergence of rogue elements in the CIA operations against Cuba, the mobsters hired to kill Castro, and disaffected Cuban exiles, from whom the Kennedy brothers withdrew their support after the Cuban missile crisis. A central figure in this drama is Sam Giancana, one of Joe Kennedy's fixers in Jack's presidential campaign, who was also party to the CIA's schemes to dispose of Castro. Fatally, the ambassador was unable to deliver on his promise that the FBI would lay off the mob after the 1960 election. Instead, Bobby Kennedy redoubled his efforts against those whom he considered "bad men". Moreover, during the final weeks of Jack's

Left: JFK relaxing with his family outside his own house in the Kennedy compound at Hyannis Port, August 1963. Above: Family friend Toni Bradlee, wife of journalist Ben Bradlee, attempts to control Caroline's pony Leprechaun, who seems intent on munching a presidential ear. JFK called out to photographer Cecil Stoughton, "Keep going, Captain, you are about to see a President being eaten by a horse." Right: JFK was an expert helmsman. Here he cuts through the bay at Hyannis Port with Bobby and Jackie in the Victura, *the boat which the ambassador had given him in 1932.*

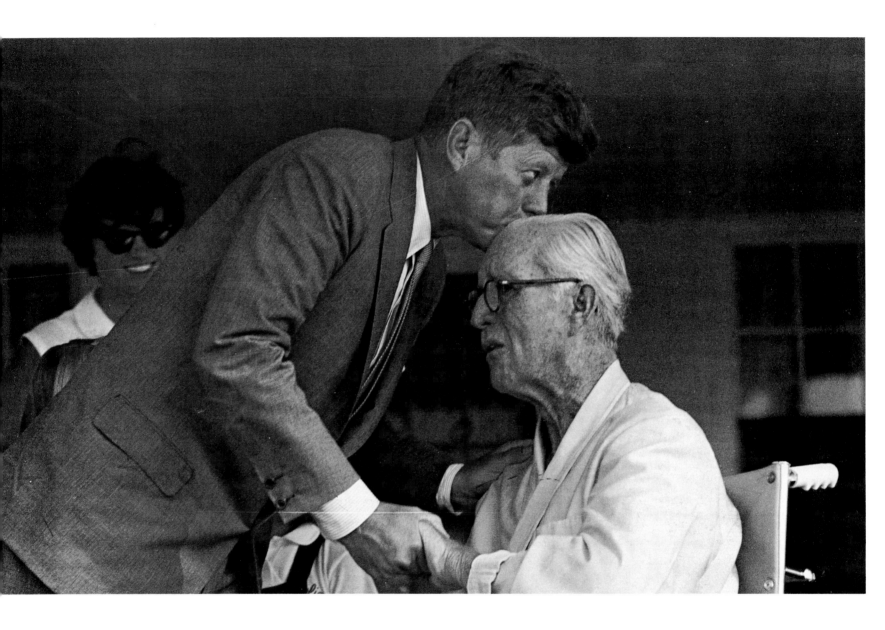

Opposite: *Jack kisses his father goodbye before boarding the presidential helicopter. For two years the ambassador had been crippled and unable to speak as the result of a stroke. Dave Powers recalls that this was the last time that the ambassador – the man who had made it all possible – saw his son alive. Powers remembers that on his way to the helicopter JFK turned back to give his father one last farewell kiss. The date was 15 November 1963, and assassination in Dallas lay just around the corner. Above: "Mrs Kennedy is organizing herself" – JFK in the parking lot of of the Hotel Texas, Fort Worth, 22 November 1963.*

Moments after the President was fatally hit in Dealey Plaza. Jackie reaches out for the hand of Secret Service agent Clint Hill. As the President's Lincoln sped away, Hill looked into the rear of the car to see instantly that much of Kennedy's head was missing and that Governor Connally, traveling with the President and also hit, was unconscious.

presidency the administration had put out secret diplomatic feelers to Castro, an initiative of which those hostile to Kennedy were fully aware. Denied a return to their squalid inheritance in Cuba, from which they milked millions in the days of the Batista regime, and smarting at what they considered a Kennedy "double cross", the mobsters and their friends contemplated revenge.

There is a terrible irony in the possibility that Jack's death flowed from the machinations of the father who made him president. When Jack died Joe Kennedy was already disabled by the stroke which in 1961 had left him paralyzed and speechless, unable to make anything more than unintelligible sounds and to endlessly repeat "No! No! No!" Isolated from the teeming Kennedy world he had created, the ambassador watched his son's funeral on the television. Shortly afterward, in a cruel misunderstanding, the flag which had draped Jack's coffin was placed over his bed as he slept. When he awoke, his screams roused everyone in the house.

In a *Newsweek* article of May 1961, Kenneth Crawford wrote, "These attractive Kennedys ... enlist our empathy. We want them to be all they seem to be." Now that Jack's heroic outline has been blurred, and in some cases entirely redrawn, by a succession of revisionist biographers, we know that the Kennedys were never what they seemed.

But the real Jack still eludes us, just as he sometimes puzzled those who knew him and wondered what lay behind the apparent frankness and charm of that flat gaze. Perhaps the original Jack Kennedy disappeared during the harrowing period in which he remade himself at the behest of his father.

The man who was president still exerts a mythic pull generated by the drama of his presidency, his physical grace and the terrible events surrounding his death. Captured on the Zapruder film, the repeated image of his head exploding as the bullets found their mark in Dealey Plaza plays on a psychic loop we can never erase. But myths can cut both ways, allowing some to see Kennedy as a hero still, others as a villain: the man who saved the world from nuclear war in the Cuban missile crisis, or the Cold War warrior who brought us all to the brink of destruction; the lost leader who would have saved America from the agony of Vietnam, or the man who set the scene for the ensuing tragedy; the devoted father or the compulsive womanizer whose recklessness sullied the office of the presidency. It is easy to forget that he was just a man, as mortal as we all are. This is how we should remember him.

Opposite: A family and a nation mourn at JFK's funeral in Washington, 25 November 1963. The President was killed three days before his son's birthday and five days before his daughter's. "He belongs to the country," Jacqueline Kennedy had said, expressing her wish for the President to be buried in the National Cemetery at Arlington rather than in the family plot in Massachusetts.

FURTHER READING

Alsop, Joseph with Platt, Adam	*I've Seen the Best of It* (New York, 1992)
Ball, George W.	'JFK's Big Moment', *New York Review of Books*, February 1992
	The Past Has Another Pattern: Memoirs (New York, 1982)
Beschloss, Michael R.	*Kennedy and Roosevelt: The Uneasy Alliance* (New York, 1980)
	The Crisis Years: Kennedy and Khrushchev, 1960-63 (New York,1991)
Brugioni, Dino A.	*Eyeball to Eyeball: The Inside Story of the Cuban Missile Crisis* (New York, 1991)
Buchan, John	*Pilgrim's Way* (published in London as *Memory Hold-the-Door*, 1940)
Burns, James MacGregor	*John Kennedy: A Political Profile* (New York,1969)
Bradlee, Ben	*Conversations with Kennedy* (New York, 1975)
Blair, Joan and Clay	*The Search for JFK* (New York, 1978)
Collier, Peter and Horowitz, David	*The Kennedys: An American Drama* (New York, 1984)
Fairlie, Henry	*The Kennedy Promise* (London, 1972)
Fay, Paul B.	*The Pleasure of His Company* (New York, 1966)
Galbraith, John Kenneth	*Ambassador's Journal, A Private Account of the Kennedy Years* (New York, 1969)
Gadney, Reg	*Kennedy* (New York, 1983)
Goodwin, Doris Kearns	*The Fitzgeralds and the Kennedys* (New York, 1987)
Halberstam, David	*The Best and the Brightest* (New York, 1972)
Kennedy, Robert Francis	*Thirteen Days* (New York, 1969)
Kennedy, Rose Fitzgerald	*Times to Remember* (New York, 1974)
Lincoln, Evelyn	*My Twelve Years with John F. Kennedy* (New York, 1965)
Manchester, William	*The Death of a President* (New York, 1967)
	The Glory and the Dream (Boston,1974)
O'Donnell, Kenneth and Powers, David	*Johnny, We Hardly Knew Ye* (Boston, 1972)
O'Neill, Tip	*Many the House* (New York, 1987)
Parmet, Herbert S.	*Jack: The Struggles of John F. Kennedy* (New York, 1980)
	JFK: The Presidency of John F. Kennedy (New York, 1983)
Lieberson, Goddard (ed)	*John Fitzgerald Kennedy ... As We Remember Him* (New York, 1965)
Reeves, Thomas C.	*A Question of Character: A Life of John F. Kennedy* (New York, 1991)
Salinger, Pierre	*With Kennedy* (New York, 1966)
Searls, Hank	*The Lost Prince: Young Joe, the Forgotten Kennedy, the Story of the Oldest Brother* (New York, 1969)
Schlesinger, Arthur Jr	*A Thousand Days: Kennedy in the White House* (Boston,1964)
	Robert Kennedy and His Times (Boston, 1978)
Sorensen, Theodore	*Kennedy* (New York, 1965)
White, Theodore H.	*The Making of the President 1960* (New York, 1964)
Whalen, Richard J.	*The Founding Father: The Story of Joseph P.Kennedy* (New York, 1965)
Wills, Garry	*The Kennedy Imprisonment: A Meditation on Power* (Boston, 1981)
Wofford, Harris	*Of Kennedys and Kings* (New York, 1980)

ACKNOWLEDGEMENTS

Except where specified below the illustrations in this book are taken from the Presidential Collection of the John Fitzgerald Kennedy Library:

75,76,77,79,80,81,83,85,87,91,121,130,131,141,143,178,183,188 - *Look Collection*, John Fitzgerald Kennedy Library; 98-99 - *Detroit Free Press*, Press Collection, John Fitzgerald Kennedy Library; 102 - *Los Angeles Times*, Press Collection, John Fitzgerald Kennedy Library; 144-5 *New York Times*, Press Collection, John Fitzgerald Kennedy Library. Images from the Presidential Collection and all the above reproduced courtesy of the John Fitzgerald Kennedy Library. 3,100,101,102,103,104,105,107,109,189 - © *Burton Berinsky Collection*, John Fitzgerald Kennedy Library, reproduced courtesy of Helene Berinsky; 93,95,97 - photographs © 1992 *Jacques Lowe*; 133 - *Camera Press*; 129,148-149 - *Popperfoto*; 186,187 - *Topham Picture Source*.

Index